PRAYER

ABOUT THE AUTHOR:

Kirpal Singh (1894-1974) of Delhi, India began, at a young age, an intense search for a true spiritual Master. For years he investigated the claims of yogis and saints representing many schools of thought. His search culminated in initiation by the great saint of Beas, Baba Sawan Singh. For twenty-four years he diligently studied under his Master's guidance, and was chosen to succeed him in the spiritual line. Thereafter, he served as a spiritual Master for twenty-six years and initiated more than 120,000 disciples throughout the world. He is the author of over twenty books on various aspects of spirituality. In addition, he served as president of the World Fellowship of Religions, and was the organizer of the World Conference on the Unity of Man. In 1974 he appointed Darshan Singh as his spiritual successor.

Sant Kirpal Singh Ji
(1894-1974)

PRAYER

Its Nature and Technique

KIRPAL SINGH

SAWAN KIRPAL PUBLICATIONS

Library of Congress Catalog: 81-50727
ISBN 0-918224-10-1

First published by Ruhani Satsang, Delhi, 1959
Second Edition, 1965
Third Edition, 1970
This Edition published by Sawan Kirpal Publications, 1981
Bowling Green, VA / Delhi, India

Printed in the United States of America

Dedicated
to the Almighty God
working through all Masters who have come
and Baba Sawan Singh Ji Maharaj
at whose lotus feet
the writer imbibed sweet elixir of
Holy Naam—the Word

Baba Sawan Singh Ji
(1858-1948)

To The Reader

*Man shall not live by bread alone, but by every
word that proceedeth out of the mouth of God.*
                                    MATTHEW 4:4

PRAYER is the salt of life and we cannot do without
it. It is ingrained in the nature of Man to pray for
the fulfillment of his wishes whatever they be. But more
often than not we do not know what we may really pray
for, how to pray, and what we may do to make our
prayer a great dynamic force as may stir up Heaven's
mercy.

The secret of a successful prayer lies not so much in
the words we use, nor in the time we devote to it, nor in
the effort that we put into it, as it lies in the concentrated
attention that we may give it at the seat of the soul so
as to make it soulful. The most natural form for a fruitful prayer is the yearning of a soul without the agency
of words, oral or mental, with the tongue of thought.
A prayer like this generates and releases such a fund of
spiritual energy that all the Cosmic Powers are attracted
and combine together, shaping out things as best as possible.

A true prayer is one continuous process, independent
of form, time and place, and leads ultimately to the stage
of *Sehaj*—a halcyon calm, a perfect equipoise and a

complete satiety, with no desire whatsoever. This then is the climax of a genuine prayer and here prayer itself ceases to be a prayer and becomes a state of being, as one gradually rises first into Cosmic Consciousness, with the Divine Will fully revealed unto him. This is the be-all and the end-all of prayer: and how to achieve it is the object of this enquiry.

At the end of the book, by way of an appendix, are collected, in classified form, specimen prayers from various Saints and Scriptures for the benefit of the interested reader.

KIRPAL SINGH

July 1, 1959
Sawan Ashram, Delhi, India

Sant Darshan Singh Ji
(1921-   )

Table of Contents

21. The Advantages of Prayer   57

22. Gradations in Prayer   59

23. What to Ask from God   62

24. Guru is the Greatest Gift of God   84

25. What One Should Ask from the Godman   88

    APPENDIX: Specimen Prayers   95

        Prayers from Kabir   100

        Ode to the Satguru   102

        Hymns of Mira   107

        From Dhani Dharam Das   109

        From Sikh Scriptures   110

        From Book of Common Prayer   136

        Prayers from Various Religions   142

    References   151

My wishes count but little:
Let Thy Will prevail.

NANAK

PRAYER

Prayer

*Prayer is the Master-Key that unlocks
the Kingdom of Heaven*

PRAYER can be defined as an anguished cry of the soul in distress or helplessness, to a Power fuller and greater than itself, for relief and comfort. It is, in the generic and commonly accepted sense, an invocation to God or Godman (a living Master), competent enough to grant solace and peace to a mind tortured by the problems of life and life's surroundings.

> *Prayer is the soul's sincere desire,*
> *Uttered or unexpressed;*
> *The motion of a hidden fire*
> *That trembles in the breast.*
>
> VISCOUNT MONTGOMERY

A worldly-wise man in this scientific age regards human life just as any other mechanical contrivance which moves and acts blindly on the lone principle of "Cause and Effect" with no guiding hand behind it. Against this mechanistic concept of man and the universe there is an organic concept as well. Without denying the principle of "Cause and Effect" that is visibly in operation in human affairs, the exponents of the organic theory see behind it the hand of God or the Law of God in and through which the principle of "Cause and Effect" is

I

at work. The Law of God then is the motor power or seed force from which every conceivable principle— scientific or ethical—springs and works out the Divine Will according to His purpose. We unfortunately see only the surface currents and cannot penetrate into the depths beneath.

In common experience we see that a worldly-wise man with all the material resources at his command is actually in a state of dire helplessness. Ever dissatisfied with what he has, he cries for more and blindly works to that end, employing all means, fair or foul, to achieve his desires. But all his riches and possessions, pelf and power, name and fame, fail to give him any degree of satisfaction. He still continues, more helpless than ever before in the face of disease, decay and death. His mind is always haunted by untold fears and imaginary horrors. With no moorings, he drifts rudderless upon the ocean of life, a prey to chance winds and waters. In this sad plight, either he flounders on the rock of suicide, or, if he escapes that, he drags on a weary existence until death comes to his rescue. But even in death he finds no comfort. He yields to it simply because he cannot help it. This is the sad story of a common man of the workaday world.

On the other hand, a really wise man also tries, like the former, to collect means of a comfortable existence; but unlike the other, these do not, in his case, form an obsession with him. Behind all his efforts, he sees the hand of God and is never bothered by success or failure in his endeavors. He leaves the result to the "Divine Will" for that alone knows what is good for him to possess. If things come to him as he desires, he does not feel elated but accepts them with sincere thanks and with a grateful heart. But if things turn the other way, he does not feel dejected, but smilingly bows down his head before the Supreme Judge who decided otherwise; and at every step he prays to God, for he knows that without His active aid, he cannot do anything by himself.

"Prayer" is, in a strict sense, another name for collecting the outgoing and wandering faculties of the mind, at the root of the mind. Like the rays of the sun, these spread out into the world, and likewise these can be withdrawn and collected at their source. A person in infatuation with a thing which he cannot get, or in distress and distraction over some calamity from which he cannot escape, sets his face toward God for success in his endeavors or comfort in his woebegone condition as the case may be. This concentration while begging for help is called prayer.

Human mind is the throne of God and hence it is, at times, termed *Kaaba*.

> *Of all the pilgrimages, the one to the human*
> *mind is the most sacred,*
> *Much better it is, to win merit here, than*
> *countless trips to Mecca.*
>
> MAULANA RUMI

As soon as a person collects himself and focuses his attention at the seat of the mind, he stirs up the mercy of God, which, in turn, fills him with strength and fortitude never experienced before. These enable him to find

a way out of the difficulty whatever it be. A will, when
concentrated, works wonders. "Where there is a will
there is a way," is a common saying. Prayer is nothing
but concentrated will falling back upon its source, the
great reservoir of power, in which are lodged all sorts
of possibilities—physical, mental and spiritual—and one
can draw upon any of these according to one's needs.
Great indeed is man. He lives in a God-made temple
along with God Himself. His very spirit is just a drop
from the Ocean of Divine Life. Between God and spirit,
there is no other obstacle but that of the veil of the
mind. If this veil were to stop fluttering in the breeze
of desires, as it does at present, the spirit could take in
directly the Cosmic Energy from its very source.

"As you think, so you become," is a common adage.
If a part thinks of the whole, it gradually begins to
imbibe the characteristics of the latter. So is the case
with the human spirit. It can gradually expand until
it becomes all-embracing from the cribbed, cabined,
cramped and cringing position that it occupies in its
present state. When freed from its entanglements—
physical, mental and causal—it triumphantly cries out:
"I am soul," or "I am as Thou art," or "I and my
Father are one" (as Christ put it).

There are two types of people in the world: first,
those who can withdraw, introvert and take inspiration
directly from the Great Power within. Secondly, those
who depend on outer aids, like churches and temples
for worship and offering prayers at altars or before idols
and statues. Some try to seek inspiration from the great
forces of Nature, like the sun, the moon, the snow-

covered hilltops, waters of the sacred rivers, as different manifestations of the One Power behind the entire Universe. Everyone according to his faith and degree of concentration gets some benefit from his mode of worship, for nothing is lost in Nature and no effort goes in vain.

Some people do not believe in the existence of God and as such have no faith in prayer, for they do not realize that God has no objective appearance and cannot be seen by the eyes of flesh.

> *O Nanak! the eyes that behold the Lord are quite different from those with which we see the world.*[1]
>
> GURU ARJAN

The truth, in fact, is that God is spirit, and can be worshiped in spirit only. We cannot worship Him with human hands and much less in handmade temples and synagogues. He dwells in the inmost depths of the human soul. He is the soul of our very soul. He is immanent in every form and not apart from forms. All colors and all patterns alike take their hue and design from Him alone. Whether we believe in Him or not, we actually live in Him and have our very being in Him.

True prayer then is the means to concentrate the wandering wits at one center—the center of the soul— to gather up the spirit currents at the still-point in the body, between and behind the eyes. Herein lies all worship, all prayers, all renunciation and all knowledge of here and hereafter. The path to salvation lies in direct touch with the Inner Power rather than to get entangled in this or that thing. "Truth is one, though sages have described it variously," is a well known Upanishadic saying. Why not then search out the Eternal Truth, of which Nanak speaks:

> *Truth was in the beginning of Creation, Truth has been the beginning of each Age, and Truth shall ever remain when all ages and creations pass away.*

> JAP JI

2. Prayer: Instinctive in Man

PRAYER is instinctive with man and no one can do without prayer at one stage or another, whatever form it may take. The faithful and the faithless, a *Momin* and a *Kafir*, a man of God and a man who has no belief in God, all pray, each one of course in his own particular way. The need for prayer generally arises when one finds himself in distress, in calamity, or in the grip of some devastating disease, or when he desires satisfaction of some unusual physical and spiritual need which he cannot otherwise fulfill, or when he wants to combat forces of adversity or darkness. In such circumstances, he feels that by his own unaided efforts he cannot secure satisfaction of his wants, and in utter helplessness he seeks strength in prayer. In everyday life we see a student seeking the aid of a teacher in the solution of some difficult problems, a patient in illness that of a physician, an employee that of his employer and so on. All these are prayers in varying degrees and forms. Again, for the satisfaction of his daily needs, a child looks up to his parents, a wife to her husband, etc.

In all trying circumstances, prayer is the last weapon in our armory. Where all human efforts fail, prayer succeeds.

> . . . *More things are wrought by prayer than*
> *this world dreams of . . .*
> . . . *For what are men better than sheep or*
> *goat,*
> *That nourish a blind life within the brain,*
> *If knowing God, they lift not their hands in*
> *prayer,*
> *Both for themselves and those they call friends.*
>
> TENNYSON

When prayer is the salt of life, we cannot do without it. But whom do we pray to? The answer naturally is, "To the One Supreme God or the Godman in whom His power resides and through whom it works in the world." All religions are in agreement on the point that prayer at the seat of the soul draws out all the latent powers of Godhood within and one can achieve spiritual beatitude through it. It is a connecting link between the Creator and His creation, between God and man. It is a supporting staff in the hands of a spiritual aspirant and a pilgrim soul cannot do without it, right from the beginning to the end of the journey, for it saves one from many a pitfall on the way and transforms the mind through and through until it shines forth and begins to reflect the light of the soul.

*Through His Grace the osprey turns into a
royal swan,
O Nanak! He may make a cygnet of a crow.*[2]

                GURU NANAK

3. Whom to Address

ONE must pray to the Lord God alone who is Omnipotent and competent to grant all wishes.

There is nothing which God cannot grant.

                KABIR

*Rich indeed is one who has Nature at his beck
and call.*[3]

                GURU ARJAN

The various gods and goddesses have a limited scope and sphere of action and so work within limitations. They themselves draw their powers from Him and may not grant the petty boons that lie within their sphere and certainly cannot grant salvation to the soul. A freed soul can grant freedom and no one else can. Guru Arjan tells us that God alone can remedy all types of maladies, no matter whether physical (like aches, ailments and various types of diseases), astral (like unforeseen and unpredictable disasters from accidents, thunder and lightning, floods and earthquakes, etc.), or causal (ingrained and·inherent evil propensities like lust, anger, greed, attachment and egoism).

*God! Thou art the dispeller of all evils and
bestower of peace,
Whosoever prays unto Thee, can have no ill.*[4]

                GURU ARJAN

*The dawn of Heaven's Light makes one a
worshiper of Truth alone,
The blossoming of loving devotion makes one
forget lifeless objects of adoration,
The knowledge of Him shows the futility of
all rites and rituals,
The manifestation of the holy light within,
distinguishes the pure from the impure.*

GURU GOBIND SINGH

Again, Guru Arjan says:

*I pray to Him who is the bestower of all bless-
ings and savior from all ills,
Shower Thy mercy, O Merciful! for then will
my efforts be well directed.*[5]

*Remember the One and sing thou His praises,
Chant His holy name and keep Him ensconced
in thy heart.
Ceaselessly meditate on His endless attributes,
and
Serve Him with all thy heart and soul.
God is one, peerless and precious,
Complete in Himself, all-pervasive and per-
meating,
Creator of the vast creation is that One.
Worship then the One and none besides,
Be saturated, body and mind, in His love,
O Nanak! through the Grace of the Master, is
that One realized.*[6]

GURU ARJAN

*If ever thou hast a wish, ask the Lord for its
fulfillment,
It shall be granted unto thee, the Master is
witness thereto.
Boundless riches come from Him and so doth
the Elixir of Life,
Merciful is the dispeller of all fears and ever
abideth with His slave.*[7]

GURU RAM DAS

*I pray to Thee, O Lord, the Lord Thou art of
my body and soul.
Nanak attributes his greatness to Thee, for
none knew him ever before.*[8]

GURU ARJAN

*Thou art the woof and warp, O Lord, and I
pray unto Thee,
For Thou art my altar, whether in pleasure or
in pain I be.*[9]

GURU RAM DAS

*In vain we pray to the people of the world full
of troubles as they are,
Pray alone to the Lord if wishest thou to cross
the ocean of life.*[10]

GURU ARJAN

In the holy Koran, it is clearly stated that God alone
need be invoked, for an invocation to Him is the only
true invocation in the correct sense of the word.

Similarly, Abraham, while denouncing his own followers, declared:

I leave you and all the gods that you worship.
I just call upon my God and I am confident
that I shall not remain empty-handed.

Again he addressed them thus:

O ye faithful, let us unite and come to a
common ground—the ground of Divinity—
and worship none else but God and consider
not anyone else on par with Him, for none
can equal Him.[11]

KORAN

The instinct of love cannot come into play unless one sees the beloved. As long as we do not see Godhead or the glory of God, we cannot have any faith in the existence of God; and without this all prayers go in vain. But *Guru* or Godman is the abode of God's Light and is a radiating center of the same. We can pray with equal efficacy to the Master, who is at one with God. Connected as he is with the Powerhouse behind him, he is equally competent to grant our desires and fulfill our wishes. It is said that,

God manifests Himself in the form of a Sadh
(a disciplined soul).[12]

GURU ARJAN

Again, the Bible tells us:

Surely the Lord God will do nothing, but he
revealeth his secret unto his servants the
prophets.[13]

In Gurbani we have:

> *God speaks through a Sadh.*
>
> GURU ARJAN

A Muslim divine tells us:

> *His (the Master's) words are Allah's (God's)
> words, though seemingly these may appear
> to be coming from a human tongue.*

A prayer to the living Master is as good as a prayer to God. One must, therefore, wholly and solely depend on the Master and turn to Him for the fulfillment of his desires.

So all prayers should be addressed to one who holds the mystery of life and death in his hands. We must have perfect faith in the living God, who lives and moves amongst us in a human form. With the attention fully focused on Him, we ought not to think of anyone else. This is the one way we can commune with Him. Kabir Sahib tells us that distance does not count in the relationship between the Master and the disciple. The two may be separated by vast oceans in between, but the very thought of the Master, in the disciple, is bound to attract the Master's attention and he can direct him (the disciple) wherever he may be. It is said of Vivekananda that when he rose to address the World Parliament of Religions in Chicago he felt diffident. He asked for a glass of water, closed his eyes for a moment, and thought of his Master (Paramhansa Ramakrishna, the sage of Dakshineshwar) and in an instant the floodgates of inspiration opened within him, and he delivered

an unprecedented and impassioned discourse lasting for
several hours. A Godman is a veritable king, and at his
door all the mighty kings of the earth bow down their
heads in humble supplication and seek the fulfillment of
their cherished desires and attainment of their otherwise unattainable ambitions.

Guru Arjan says in this context:

> *He has within his controlling power all the*
> *potentates,*
> *Nay, the vast creation itself is under his sway.*
> *His will reigns supreme everywhere,*
> *And nothing lies outside his Divine Will;*
> *O offer thy prayer to thy Master alone,*
> *For he shall fulfill all thy heart's desires.*
> *His seat is in the highest heavens, and*
> *Devotion unto him lies in communion with His*
> *Word.*
> *All-pervading, He is complete in Himself,*
> *And His light shines in every heart,*
> *His remembrance dispels all sorrows,*
> *Even the angel of death does not come near*
> *his devotee.*
> *The dead come to life by the Power of His*
> *Word, and*
> *The lowliest and the lost are received and*
> *honored.*
> *O Nanak! thy prayer has been heard and*
> *accepted, and*
> *Through the Grace of the Master, His Light*
> *has been made manifest within.*[15]

A Godman has within his grasp all that one may need—
the gifts of *Dharma, Artha, Kaama* and *Moksha* (the
merits of righteousness, earthly riches and possessions,
fulfillment of wishes and desires, and salvation itself).

> *If one wants any of the four great boons*
> *He must take to the service of a Sadh.*
> *If one wishes to have riddance from affliction*
>   *and sorrow,*
> *One must commune with the Word, in the*
>   *depths of one's soul.*
> *If one is after name and fame,*
> *One must lose his ego in the company of a*
>   *saint.*
> *If one be afraid of the pangs of birth and*
>   *death,*
> *One must seek shelter at the lotus feet of a*
>   *saint.*[16]

GURU ARJAN

From the above it is abundantly clear that we must go
in prayer unto God or a Godman and after being able
to commune with Him, we should depend on Him alone
and not on any other power; for He alone is capable
of drawing one out from the mighty swirls and eddying
pools of mind and matter, and of applying a healing
balm to the lacerated hearts torn by wild desires and
temptations. He is the strength of the weak, the sheet-
anchor in the storm and stress of life and a haven of
safety for the homeless. His glance of Grace soothes the
broken hearts.

A perfect Master attends to the heart,
And from heart to heart, a life impulse darts.

BHAI NANDLAL

It behooves a disciple to unhesitatingly unburden his mind to his Master and place his difficulties before him, wherever he may be, for the Master is above time and space and can attend to his disciple's tale of woe.

Rip open thy mind before thy Master;
Cast aside all thy cunning and cleverness, and
Take refuge, body and soul, at His feet.[17]

GURU ARJAN

In the holy Koran, we have:

Except him, there is none who listens to the
woeful tale of the distressed and the ago-
nized cry of the helpless and renders solace
unto him.

Christ's remarks in this behalf are significant enough:

That whatsoever ye shall ask of the Father in
my name, He may give it you.[18]

If ye shall ask anything in my name, I will
do it.[19]

Since God or a Godman is the treasure-house of all blessings, we must offer our prayer to either of them and to none else.

4. A Direct Appeal to God Within

IN WORLDLY matters, we do seek the help of persons who are more intelligent and capable than we are. We also offer prayers for aid to God—the greatest power conceivable—and that, no doubt, is a correct approach to the difficult and baffling problems which confront us every day in the course of our lives. But to regard that Omnipotent Power as something separate and apart from us, and to appeal to Him as to an outside benefactor, is assuredly a sorrowful mistake which is made by us; for He is the very soul of our soul, and is ever working within and without us, and we, in fact, live and have our very being in Him. The secret of success lies in direct prayer and appeal to the power within, as these bear sure fruit and in abundance. We do a great injustice both to Him and to ourselves when we think of God residing on snow-capped mountains, or under the depths of sacred rivers and water-springs, or in temples and mosques, or in churches and synagogues, or in this or that holy place. Limited as we are in time, space, and causation, we try to limit the Limitless within the narrow grooves that imagination can conceive of. Such belief on our part and consequent frustrations that result therefrom not infrequently tend to make us sceptical of Him.

When the reservoir of all power is in each one of us, we can, by a dip therein, become spiritually great and powerful. As physical exercises make us robust and strong physically, so do spiritual exercises awaken in us latent spiritual powers. By means of these we can pull up the sluice-gates and thus flood our very being with Divine Currents. When a person becomes Divinized or Divinity Personified, the very Nature, which is the handmaid of God, begins to dance at his beck and call to fulfill all his needs and requirements.

A strong will does forge ahead and make a way for itself. We do, at times, by praying to some supposed powers without, succeed in our endeavors. Such success is in fact due to a little concentrated effort on our part rather than to any outside agency. In this way we not only deceive ourselves, but gradually perpetuate the self-deception to the extent that in course of time it becomes a part of us, and we cannot but look upon God as something extraneous to us, and the worst of it is that we do not at all come in contact with the untold treasures of Divinity that lie within us and constitute our own heritage. It is only after the inner contact with Him has been established that we can truly understand His pervasiveness in the Universe and see His glory everywhere. Without this direct perception and first-hand experience of Him within, our conception of God is just hearsay or bookish and hence erroneous, and our prayers to Him a meaningless jargon.

5. Prayer and Effort

PRAYER and effort go cheek by jowl. We pray to God for what? For the success of our endeavors. Should we wish for a thing, we must try for it, and alongside our efforts to achieve it pray that God may grant it. Prayer is just the last weapon and a sure one that comes to our aid. Where all human efforts fail, prayer succeeds.

> . . . *More things are wrought by prayer, than this world dreams of.*
>
> TENNYSON

As a bird cannot fly on one wing only nor a chariot

move on one wheel, so effort and prayer must go together if we want success in all our ventures. One of them by itself can achieve nothing. As long as a person is not fully Divinized, or in other words does not become a conscious co-worker with the Supreme Power by understanding His Will, he cannot do without endeavor, for God helps those who help themselves.

A mere prayer without endeavor seldom bears fruit. Just take the instance of a boy who is late for school. If he were to sit down on the roadside to pray, he would be running against time. If he wants to gain time, he must run and it is possible that even if he be late his teacher may forgive him because of the effort he has made to reach there in time. To have a ruling passion for an objective and to work hard for achieving the same is the right type of prayer in the truest sense of the word. Effort should be combined with prayer, for mere lip service to reach the goal will not help much. In all sincerity one should pray and indeed the very striving for a thing with heart and soul is the greatest prayer and is bound to fructify. In all trials and tribulations, one must try to rid himself of his weariness and pray to God that He may help him in his endeavors. This is the only right attitude. In the Koran, it is said that when Moses and Aaron prayed for victory over the Pharaoh, God, accepting their prayers, commanded them to stand steadfast and not to follow the tracks of those who were ignorant of the Reality. Moses too commanded his followers to be true and seek the help of God. In moments of storm and stress, never grow disheartened, especially as you stand on the bedrock of

God and Godman. If, in spite of this, you fail in your endeavors, then take that failure as coming from God for your good.

6. The Essentials of Prayer

If ye then, being evil, know how to give good gifts unto your children, how much more shall your Father which is in Heaven give good things to them that ask Him.[20]

CHRIST

A PRAYER never goes in vain. A cry from the heart is always heard and attended to; but how, and in what manner, depends on the Will of God.

A prayer of a devotee never goes in vain.[21]

Whatever a devotee asks of Him, that cannot but happen. [22]

*He doth grant whatever is asked of Him,
O Nanak! the words of a devotee prove true here and hereafter.*[23]

GURU ARJAN

In the Sikh scriptures it is mentioned that the Father God, ordained that He would freely give whatsoever His children may ask of Him:

The Ever-kind Father has pledged to fulfill what His children may desire.[24]

GURU ARJAN

The Holy Koran likewise vouchsafes this very idea when it states:

God has said, call upon Me, and I shall accept
thy call.

And again:

O Rasul! whenever any person enquires of
Me, tell him that I reside in him and I listen
to his prayers whatever the same may be.

In the Gospel of St. Matthew we have:

Ask and it shall be given you; seek and ye shall
find; knock and it shall be opened unto you:
For everyone that asketh receiveth; and he
that seeketh findeth; and to him that
knocketh it shall be opened.[25]

In actual experience, however, we find that most of our prayers do not bear any fruit. We have, therefore, to study the question critically as to what type of prayer is acceptable to God, and how that prayer is offered, and why all prayers are not accepted. For success in prayers there are certain essential prerequisites:

(*i*) *Faith in God* is the root cause of success. We may deceive ourselves and those around us, but we cannot deceive the inner power—God. In offering prayers, we run a great handicap race. We are not true in our thoughts, words and deeds. There is, in fact, no harmony among the three. We depend too much on our own cunning, maneuvering and scheming. We have no confidence in God and His powers. Our prayers do not arise from the depths of our soul. Far from being an anguished cry, we mechanically utter a few words of hurried prayer. It is just doing a lip service to God which is not even skin deep. No wonder then, that these perfunctory and ceremonial prayers for form's sake go in vain and are not heard. We must realize that God is great and that He knows our inmost thoughts and the very working of our mind, and have faith in His munificence, for:

> *He knows what lies within the folds of our mind,*
> *And is fully aware of the afflictions of all: the virtuous and the vile.*
>
> GURU GOBIND SINGH

(*ii*) *Surrender to God.* With faith in God, the next step automatically is to surrender one's all at the feet of God. When the little self loses itself in the greater Self, the latter works and acts for and on behalf of the former. In such a case there hardly remains the need of actual prayer.

> *O mind! be acceptable to thy Lord,*
> *Be ye all humble and lowly unto Him.*[26]
>
> GURU ARJAN

(*iii*) *Love for God* is another prerequisite for successful prayers. We ought to be grateful to Him for what He has done for us without our asking, before we ask Him for further boons. We must love and respect His commandments and strictly follow them. We bow down a thousand times before Him but we do not, unfortunately, take His words seriously. Little do we realize that He is not apart from His words.

If ye love me, keep my commandments.[27]

*If ye abide in me, and my words abide in you,
ye shall ask what ye will, and it shall be
done unto you.*[28]

CHRIST

*Delight yourself also in the Lord; and He shall
give the desires of thine heart.*[29]

THE PSALMS

(*iv*) *Right attitude* is another essential for expecting
favors of God. Right attitude may be considered in
relation both to God and to man. "He that turneth
away his ear from hearing the law, even his prayers
shall be abomination."

*And whatsoever we ask, we receive of Him,
because we keep His commandments, and
do those things that are pleasing in His sight.*

Again, if we want God to forgive our trespasses, we
must be prepared to forgive freely the trespasses of
others.

*And forgive us our debts, as we forgive our
debtors. . . .
For if ye forgive men their trespasses, your
heavenly Father will also forgive you:
But if ye forgive not men their trespasses, neither will your Father forgive your trespasses.*[30]

CHRIST

(*v*) *Fear of God.* We do not live in fear of the Lord. He is the very soul of our souls but we shamelessly do things in secret as if He knows them not. We feel ashamed to do a sinful act in the presence of a toddler of tender years, but have not even that much regard for the King of kings enthroned within us and looking not only to all our deeds but even reading our thoughts and knowing the drift of our instincts and propensities lying in the limbo of our subconscious mind. His fear alone can make us fearless of the world, but unfortunately we live in a state of perpetual fear of all and sundry and go about cringing petty favors here and there.

Like as a father pitieth his children, so the Lord pitieth them that fear him.[31]

THE PSALMS

Lord, I believe; help thou mine unbelief.[32]

ST. MARK

(*vi*) *Purification.* Purity of body, mind and soul is the most important factor in winning the love of the Lord. It may be considered in three different stages—Repentance, Forgiveness and Abstention.

(a) REPENTANCE. Nothing under heaven is perfect and each one of us has his own weaknesses. Sin has come to man as a heritage from Adam. Mind in man is the agent of the Negative Power, and it misses no opportunity to tempt man against God. In daily life we slip at every step. Our best resolves turn into airy nothings when temptations assail us. Unaided we cannot possibly escape from the cunning wiles, subtle snares and wild clutches of *Kal* or the Lord of Time, i.e., the mind. It is only the saving arm of the Master that can protect us and rid us of its terrible onslaughts. But every time that we fall a prey to temptations we must realize our weakness and sincerely repent for what we have done.

(b) FORGIVENESS. Repentance, though good in itself, cannot alter the past. Each act of omission or commission leaves its indelible impress upon the mind and singles us out for its reaction or fruit. In this way countless Karmic impressions go on accumulating day in and day out, making additions to our *Sanchit Karmas* (a vast storehouse of unfructified actions). Nobody can escape from this tremendous load which has a far-reaching effect, extending sometimes to hundreds of lives and over. Is there no remedy then, to burn away the powder magazine before it blows us up? The saints tell us that there is a way and a sure one indeed. Prayer for forgiveness is a positive weapon in the hands of a sinner. There is hope for everybody including the sinners. Saints come into the world to save the sinners and the lost. An association with a Master-soul goes a long way in liquidating the Karmic account. While He forgives in His Saving Grace our daily lapses, He at the same time enjoins abstention from repetition of the same. "So far and no further," is their admonition. "Go and sin no more," was the usual advice with Christ and Master Sawan Singh too, who used to advise his disciples to make a halt wherever they were and to sin no more.

The past actions can be washed off, provided we refrain from sowing any more of the dragon's teeth.

(c) ABSTENTION. While repentance and forgiveness help us in escaping the effect of *Kriyaman* or day-to-day acts, we have yet to guard against future repetitions. No purificatory process can help us through unless we put a stop to the incessant round of the Karmic wheel, which gains momentum from our every act.

At times a magistrate may award a lesser penalty for a crime but that may not ennoble the criminal. In the dispensation of the Master, there is always the stern admonition which is so necessary an element in keeping a person on his guard. He has to wash a sinner clean so as to fit him for his journey Homeward. Like a Master-sculptor, he has to chisel hard to bring shape and form out of a formless piece of stone.

In brief, it is necessary that we must first of all mould our life according to the instructions of the Master, and feel a genuine delight in thinking of Him. Secondly, we must understand His Will and pray for those things that are to His liking; and thirdly, we must learn to accept smilingly His decrees whatever they be.

Last but not least, love is the soil on which life thrives the most. Lover gives and never takes favors. If one tries to live a godly life, all God's favors automatically flow down to him. One who loves God need not ask for any favor. It is enough for us to dedicate our very life to Him and become His bound slaves. It is up to Him to treat us as He wishes. To live in His Holy Presence is its own reward and there can be no reward greater and richer than this.

> *Downright heresy it is to pray,*
> *To ask God to take the calamity away.*
>
> MAULANA RUMI
>
> *Thy frowns are fairer far*
> *Than the smiles of many maidens are.*
>
> COLERIDGE
>
> *There is exhilarating sweetness*
> *Even in thy frowns, O Master.*[33]
>
> GURU ARJAN

7. Hurdles in the Way of Prayer

SOME feel that when God knows even the innermost secrets of our minds, wherein lies the need for prayer? Some others think that when God is to grant a gift for the asking, we may in ignorance ask for things that may ultimately be harmful or injurious to us and we may have to repent for our folly. Still others believe that God, who is more than our earthly father, knowing what is good for His children would provide that without our asking and keep back that which may be detrimental to our interest. Despite all these arguments, the saints insist on offering prayers.

Doubtless God knows our needs:

> *Your Father knoweth what things ye have need*
> *of, before ye ask Him.*[34]
>
> CHRIST

> *His greatness lies in His Omniscience.*[35]
>
> GURU ARJAN

He knows the secret of every heart,
And what lies hidden underneath.

GURU GOBIND SINGH

My Kirdgaar (Creator) knows my needs much
better than I do.

A MUSLIM DIVINE

Still the underlying object in offering prayer is that *we* may know and understand our needs, be prepared for the fulfillment of the same when the time comes and be thankful to Him.

We are thy children, O Master,
Grant thou the gift of right understanding.[36]

To the ignorant children, Father giveth the
light.[37]

GURU RAM DAS

Sometimes it might seem that our prayers for riddance from calamities are not heeded, but in all certainty we do get from them fortitude enough to withstand the calamities and strength to successfully combat them without feeling their sting and their pinching effect.

8. How to Overcome Inner Difficulties

HEART is the pulpit for offering prayer and must, therefore, be cleaned and purified before we engage in prayer.

(i) *Purity of heart* consists in respectful and humble attitude toward God free from all cares and anxieties of the world.

The All-knowing Himself sets everything right,
To Him, O Nanak! offer ye thy prayer.[38]

GURU ANGAD

With folded hands offer thy prayers.[39]

GURU ARJAN

(*ii*) *Humility* born of helplessness, coupled with confidence and faith in Him.

(*iii*) *Loving Devotion.* Next we have to still the mind, to make it free from the mental oscillations that continuously pull it this way and that. To achieve stillness of the mind we have to find within some center or pole to which it may be drawn time and again, so that gradually we succeed in stilling the mind at will. Until such ground is found, an aspirant is in a very delicate and slippery state. As he withdraws from the outer world and its associations and waits for the dawn of the new world, he is haunted by countless seed impressions hitherto lying buried in the depth of unconsciousness. One can free himself from these either by right contemplation or by seeking aid through prayer to the Power within. The surest and the easiest way to cross over these hurdles is to think of the form of the Master and to fix one's attention in that form. This "tapping inside" or "knocking," as it grows continuous and steady, gradually forces open the "Way in," bringing to view endless vistas of spiritual visions and rapturous strains of Divine Symphonies.

Again there are myriads of obstacles in the inner path. Sometimes an aspirant gets no response to his prayers and begins to doubt their efficacy. At other times far

THE THREE TYPES OF PRAYER

removed from God, he finds himself in a strange and vast stillness and feels his own vibrations. Others get entangled in the deep darkness behind the eyes and cannot penetrate into the Beyond. So bewildering and complicated are these regions of darkness and silence that one feels he has lost his way. In spite of his best efforts, he totters over and over again, tries to stand on his legs but slips over. This is indeed a very sad and delicate situation. By his unaided efforts he cannot safely come out of this labyrinth. It is in such weird and eerie surroundings that instructions from a Master-soul can be of avail to him. These are just a few of the countless difficulties with which this path is strewn. The Negative Power has a regular network of pitfalls to thwart designs even of the wisest and wariest of souls and by all kinds of wiles tries to ambush the weary traveler on the path. Its triumph lies in keeping the *Jivas* or embodied souls entirely in its clutches so that its sway over them remains undiminished and its glory undimmed. One can escape these dark forces only through the help of one who has himself conquered them, for such forces live in fear of him and do not molest a soul that is in league with him. The long arm of the Master and his strong hand can lead a *Jiva* unscathed through all dangers with which the inner path is beset at every step.

9. *The Three Types of Prayer*

THERE are three ways of offering a prayer:
(*i*) *Vocal or oral*: that is to say a prayer offered by means of tongue or words of mouth. It consists in repeat-

ing some set prayer as recorded in scriptures or as given by this or that *Mahatma* as a "model prayer." Some feel that such prayers are not of much consequence. A prayer in fact is not a mere repetition of particular words but an anguished cry of an individual soul arising from its deepest depths. Such oral prayers may be likened to borrowed clothes which never fit the borrower. As models these are very valuable and we should try to make such impassioned appeals directly from the inner-most recesses of our mind, truly depicting our feelings and emotions.

(*ii*) *Mental*: A prayer may be repeated by the tongue of thought alone. This can be done only when one can prepare a suitable ground for it within himself. One must see the presence of God and be able to concentrate his thoughts before offering a thanksgiving to Him, making free and frank confessions of all his shortcomings and seeking His aid in all his endeavors. It is an art and like any other art requires a great deal of patience and steadfastness, as is necessary in learning music or painting. To start with, the mind has to be trained and stilled by constant thought of the Master, which works like a goad (the steel rod used by *Mahouts* or elephant drivers for keeping the animal under control). After offering such a prayer one must for some time wait for His grace or blessedness, which "descends like a gentle dove," says Christ. With it also comes peace that thrills one throughout from head to foot. Once a person tastes of this he feels a perfect satiation within himself. The infatuation of the world with its wondrous charms falls off like a discarded and a long-forgotten thing in the limbo of the past. In the world, he is now no longer of the world. What a wondrous change indeed! Some people consider this as the be-all and end-all of spirituality. But this is not the case. This change in outlook is but a precursor or a harbinger of the advent of the luminous form of the Master and much more thereafter.

(*iii*) *Spiritual*: For true spirituality, a *Sadhak* has yet to wait and watch. As he continues his *Sadhna*, he occasionally transcends his physical body and meets the Master in his self-refulgent form. Thence onward countless vistas of spiritual scenes unfold themselves before his inner vision. These are beyond description. While yet a denizen of this world, he gets an access to higher regions, from whence come nothing but blessedness. Here he gets dyed through and through in the true color of pure spirituality. Now he is no more "worldly-wise" as he used to be, but is charged with spirituality. He is altogether transformed into a person established in his Divinity or God-head. This may be termed *mystical prayer*. In this type of prayer an aspirant has nothing to do. It is all wrought by the Master. Once he takes charge of the soul, it becomes his responsibility to work out this transformation by gradually eliminating all traces of dross and converting the soul into pure gold. Even a most elementary experience of this stage sets at rest all doubts and misgivings. It is enough to awaken a soul into Cosmic Awareness, and from then onward it is established in its own and is no longer a prey to scepticism. In its naked pristine glory it cries out—"I am the soul" or "I am as Thou art" or "I am *Brahm*."

10. Loud Prayers

PRAYERS when uttered loudly do for the time being work like a lever in lifting the mind upward and bring about a sobriety, but as we do not understand their proper value and significance, these do not help in preparing the ground for raising the spiritual super-structure. On the contrary we often feel entangled in public applause and approbation. The result, more often than not, is that we fall an easy prey to self-deception. As these do not come from the depth of the soul, they sound hollow without a single true ring in them. They may be used to capture the imagination of an audience for the moment, but do no ultimate good to those engaged in it, either as performers or as listeners. These at times create physical sensation and bring about a trance but do not lead to Conscious Awareness, which can only come with Self-knowledge. God cannot be cowed down by loud and strong words nor does He need them. He is the very soul of our soul and can hear the faintest and feeblest tread of an ant. He knows our wants even more than we do, and long before we even feel them. The riches of spirituality do not at all come with loud professions or protestations. A prayer in the deep silence of the mind and uttered with the tongue of thought alone is capable of bearing any fruit. The rest is all in vain.

> Call upon thy God in all humility and in all silence.
>
> You need not shout, for He knows everything.
>
> KORAN

He hears an ant's call before he does the
trumpet of an elephant.[40]

GURU GOBIND SINGH

11. *Individual and Public Prayers*

IN INDIVIDUAL prayer, there is of course no need to utter words loudly. One has just to change the course of one's thoughts from one channel to another. In it, mental *Simran* is quite enough.

What is there in the quest of God?
Transplant the mind and see Him in all.

SHAH INAYAT

In public prayers we generally lose sight of real personal emotions and in spite of ourselves drift into hyperbole. In a prayer like this, there is no harmony between the mind and the tongue. Divorced from personal feelings, we are thinking only of the public applause of the moment. All the time we try to play upon the feelings of the audience, so as to draw more offerings from their pockets or tears from their eyes or words of praise for our accomplishment. These are more or less ceremonial prayers, mostly offered on the occasion of *Urs* or anniversary of the birth or death of various saints. Both *Qawwalis* among the Muslims and *Kirtans* among the Hindus fall into this category.

These set prayers are simply the outpourings of devotees in the past and not the spontaneous emotional outbursts of those who recite them, and as such are not likely to be accepted, nor do they bear any appreciable fruit or make any lasting impression on the participants on such occasions, whether the singers or the hearers. An arrow that does not take its flight right from the archer's bow-string, strung well down to the chest, hardly hits the target. Similarly, mere oral prayers, not coming out of the depths of the soul, fail to reach the Godman, who is also the very soul of our soul and is already aware of our needs more than we ourselves are.

12. Congregational Prayers

THE same may be said of congregational prayers which too fall under the above head. These are offered in temples and mosques, churches and synagogues, gurdwaras and other sacred places. The man at the pulpit gives the sermon and the audience mechanically hears it or he reads a prayer and the congregation just repeats it in a chorus. Except for some honorable exceptions, the rest just walk in for the weekly or monthly service, as the case may be, for form's sake. If such prayers do not create in us a longing for God, they avail nothing. This is the most elementary service that is expected from such prayers and if that too is not achieved, nothing is gained therefrom.

Such services, if conducted on proper lines, can do a lot of good to the people. We may pray in all humility for the welfare of humanity in general, which is a universal cause and dear to God. It is a powerful instrument that has been responsible for building nations and welding together societies.

O Nanak! great is His name.
May there be welfare of all under Thy Will,
  O Lord.

                              GURU NANAK

   O God! put us on the right path,
   Make us steadfast in faith,
   Grant us mercy, O Allah,
   None is more merciful than Thee.

O God! forgive us our trespasses,
And ignore our high-handedness,
Make us true in Thy Path,
And grant us victory over the unbelievers and
  the unfaithful.

                                   KORAN

The object of such prayers is either to ennoble ourselves
or to benefit the audience or to tell God of universal
sufferings or some needs of humanity in general or, in
the last resort, to ingratiate and push ourselves into
public favor by a show of religiosity. Prayers offered and
services conducted with the last of these motives are, of
course, not only quite useless but definitely harmful and
must therefore be avoided at all costs.

   In Sura Baqar of the Koran, it is stated:

   O God! if we err either in our endeavor or in
   practice, do not call Thou us on that ac-
   count; but forgive us our shortcomings.
   O God! never put us to hard trials and never
   impose on us restrictions and obligations as
   were ordained in times past.

*O God! do not put a heavy load on us which
we may not have the strength to bear.*

*O God! forgive us our transgressions and
shower Thy blessings on us, for Thou art
our Lord and Master; to whom may we
turn except unto Thee. Grant us Thy victory
and glory against the unbelievers and the
unfaithful.*

13. Place for Prayer

FOR prayer one needs no specific place. It grows best
and thrives most on a leavened heart. All that is
needed is a quiet place, free from the hubbub of the
world or other distracting factors. It may be done within
doors or without. Even one's sleeping room can serve
the purpose or just a part of it if the whole be not
available. In the absence of any place at home, one
may walk down to a temple or a mosque, a church or a
synagogue, for all such places are meant to satisfy this
need of the public. If none of these are near at hand,
one can by himself while walking, sitting, or lying down
along a river bank or a mountain side, do *Simran* as
ordained by the Master and commune with God and
place before Him his inner feelings. Of course the entire
world is God's creation and can be used as such.

*This world is the abode of God, and God truly
lives in the world.*[41]

GURU ANGAD

Blessed becomes the place where one sits down to pray. The whole earth is sacred and one may offer his prayer wherever he likes.

> *Mosque is the Earth and as holy it is,*
> *Pray ye the faithful when the time comes,*
> *Care not for the place wherever it be.*
>   ALAMSAEEN

God has created the whole world and He is the Lord of it all. He does not live in temples and mosques made by human hands. He, being spirit, can be worshiped in spirit only.

> *God that made the world and all things there-*
> *in, seeing that He is Lord of Heaven and*
> *Earth, dwelleth not in temples made with*
> *hands.*[42]
>   ST. PAUL

> *All is holy where devotion kneels.*
>   O. W. HOLMES

> *God is the Master of East and West*
> *Turn whichsoever side thou may,*
> *God shall look thee in the face,*
> *For He pervades in all the space.*[43]
>   KORAN

Human body is the temple of God, and it befits man to worship God in the God-made temple in which He resides. We on the contrary run out to man-made temples and mosques outside, to offer our prayers.

Know ye not that ye are the temple of God,
and that the spirit of God dwelleth in you?[44]

ST. PAUL

This body is the temple of God (Hari Man-
dir),
The true pearl of Jnana comes to shine in it.[45]

GURU AMAR DAS

Thy mind is the mosque,
Let thou be the worshiper therein.

A MUSLIM DIVINE

God can be best worshiped in the body. One need not
wander from place to place like a shuttlecock. All glory
and beauty lies within you. Outside the human body all
structures are made of water and clay. The Vedas, the
Puranas, the Koran and the Gospel all repeat the same
tale.

The beloved is in the House,
I search for Him high and low without.
While the pitcher full of water stands beside,
Woe unto me for wandering athirst.

A MUSLIM DIVINE

But thou when thou prayest, enter into thy
closet, and when thou hast shut thy door
pray to thy Father which is in secret; and
thy Father, which seeth in secret, shall re-
ward thee openly.[46]

CHRIST

Here a question might arise as to why God, who is in

the body, is not visible to us. It may be explained that
our eyes of flesh can see material things only. They are
too gross to behold the Divine Glory of the most subtle.
Unless the power of vision comes into conformity with
the density of the object, we cannot see the object. It
is, therefore, only the Inner Eye that can, when opened,
see Him.

> *Different are the eyes, O Nanak,*
> *That behold the vision of God.*[47]
>
> GURU ARJAN

> *O remove the scales from my eyes,*
> *And show me the face of the True One.*
>
> KABIR

Again:

> *Rise up to the level of God,*
> *Then alone shalt thou see Him.*[48]

> *When thou closest the ten outlets of thy body,*
> *The Light of God shall shine in thee.*[49]
>
> GURU ARJAN

> *If therefore thine eye be single, thy whole body*
> *shall be full of light.*[50]
>
> CHRIST

True prayer consists in withdrawing the spirit within
with a pure mind and fully devotional attitude. Such a
prayer cannot but bear fruit in abundance and in no
time.

14. Prerequisites in Prayer

NEED OF GODMAN. As prayer is to be addressed to someone, it is but necessary that we must first have a firm belief in the existence of the Being whom we address. We have as yet no experience of God, and have therefore no conception of Him nor of His powers. Our knowledge of Him, however little it may be, is a secondary one, derived from the study of books or heard from persons as ignorant of Him as we are. In such a state we can contemplate nothing. But there may be a person who may have a direct knowledge of God and be inwardly in tune with the Infinite. There is a peculiar charm in his company. His weighty words of wisdom at once sink deep into the mind. His utterances, charged with His power, have a magnetic influence. One feels a kind of serenity and an inward calm in his holy presence. He does not reason of God. He simply talks of Him with authority, because he has a firsthand knowledge of Him and consciously lives in Him every moment of his life. Such a person may be termed a Prophet, a Messiah, or a Godman. The Gospel tells us that God speaks through His Prophets or the chosen ones. It is but a natural thing. Man alone can be a teacher of man, and for God's science we must have some Godman to teach us that. *Sant Satguru* is the pole from where God's Light is reflected. From him alone we can know of the Path leading to God; and he can be a sure guide who can be depended upon, in weal or woe, both here and hereafter.

He that hath seen me, hath seen the Father . . .
Believe me that I am in the Father, and the
Father in me.[51]

CHRIST

From what has been said above, it naturally follows
that Godman or *Sant Satguru* is the right person to be
approached in the first instance and to whom all our
prayers should be addressed. Faith is the keynote of
success in all our endeavors. We must, then, have firm
and full faith in the competency of the Master. With
love and humility we must make an approach to him
if we want to make a beginning in Spiritual Science.
We must pray to him sincerely from the depth of our
heart. We should think it fortunate indeed if in his
grace he accepts us for imparting knowledge of *Para
Vidya*—the Science of knowledge of Self and knowledge
of God—which in fact is the seed-knowledge from which
all knowledge springs.

(*ii*) *Complete Absorption.* The next essential in this
connection is complete absorption. While offering prayer
we must forget everything else, including our body and
our bodily relations. Singleness of purpose is a *sine qua
non* for hitting the target. It is common knowledge that
one cannot serve two Masters at one time. We have to
choose between God and Mammon and then forget the
other. One by one we have to slip through the various
sheaths enveloping the soul like funeral shrouds in their
folds. The spirit is a living entity and cannot move
ahead unless it discards the material appendages in
which it is wrapped—physical, mental and causal. By

complete absorption these drop off one by one of their own accord, leaving the spirit free for flights in the spiritual regions. Mohammedans call this absorption *Fana-fil-Sheikh*, which ultimately leads to *Fana-fil-Allah*, thus completing the journey from *Fana* to *Baqa* (from death to immortality).

(*iii*) *Truthfulness and Contentment.* Our prayers can be fruitful only when we are true to ourselves in all aspects of life. We must have right thoughts, right aspirations, right contemplation, right livelihood and right conduct. Purity in thought, word and deed must precede everything else. Righteousness, chastity and truthfulness are all closely associated with and actually spring from *Brahmcharya* (self-control), which is a great motive force in life. It is on the bedrock of *Brahmcharya* that all these things grow and bear fruit.

Contentment is an active aid in controlling the wandering faculties of the mind. Unless mental oscillations stop and stillness is achieved we cannot offer a true and sincere prayer. A stilled mind alone can reflect God's Light when it may dawn.

> *God is attracted swift and sure,*
> *With prayer from mind contented and pure.*[52]
>
> GURU NANAK

> *To thine own self be true and then it must*
> *follow, as night the day, thou canst not be*
> *false to any man.*
>
> SHAKESPEARE

(*iv*) *Sincere and stirring sensation.* Prayer must arise

from the depths of the soul. It should not be a vain repetition of empty words with little meaning in them. What we pray for we must really wish for, not only intellectually but from the very core of our being. It must churn the very soul to its depths and the music of prayer should come out and tingle from the very nerves, tissues and fibres of the entire frame making us unmindful and oblivious of everything else beside the sweet music of the soul.

> *O Kabir! why to the minaret goest the Imam*
> *for a call, for God is not deaf,*
> *Why not address thy call to the mind so that it*
> *goeth within.*

(*v*) *Spontaneity*. A prayer being the cry of the soul in agony is most beautiful and most natural when it gushes forth spontaneously like a spring of cool water from the bowels of the Earth. It needs no embellishments of particular words and peculiar phrases. On the contrary, such adornments mar the true beauty of free expression, and very frequently the man of prayer is imperceptibly drawn in and imprisoned in the net of verbiage. All this makes a prayer artificial—a product of deliberate art divorced from feelings. Such prayers make us false to ourselves and are not at all beneficial. God is concerned with genuine emotions expressed in howsoever simple words and not with set speeches, vain repetitions, ostentatious phraseology and learned expostulations.

Maulana Rumi has given us a beautiful illustration of a loving prayer that a simple and unsophisticated

shepherd boy was muttering in his own humble way as
Prophet Moses passed by him. He was saying:

> *O God! where art Thou? I would like to serve
> Thee. I would knit for Thee woolen gar-
> ments and comb Thy hair. I would like to
> serve Thee with milk, curd, cheese and clari-
> fied butter, tend Thee in Thine illness, kiss
> Thy hands and massage Thy feet. I would
> like to make a sacrifice of all my sheep and
> goats for Thy sake.*

These words of the shepherd boy sounded as heresy to
the Prophet, who in a rage began to reprimand the boy
saying: "Shut up your mouth, O infidel. Why are you
talking like a fool? Withdraw your insolent words or
else God will curse us with hell-fires for your blasphemy.
God is not a human being and He does not stand in
need of any of the things that you offer Him. He is a
spirit, without any hands and feet, and you have insulted
Him with your idle talk." Stung to the quick, the simple-
hearted boy tore his clothes, ran to the wilderness and
wept bitterly for having incurred the displeasure of God.
In the intensity of his agony he lost his consciousness,
and behold, he saw within him the Light of God and
heard a sweet and kind voice assuring him that all his
prayers, sincere as they were, were acceptable to God
and He was greatly pleased with him for his offerings.
On the other hand, when Moses went into his wonted
meditation, he felt that God was sorely vexed with him
for having driven a loving soul away from Him. God
reprimanded him,

*You came into the world for uniting people
unto Me, and not for separating those who
were one with Me,*

and spake thus:

Everyone remembers Me in his own words and
according to his own inner feelings. I have accepted
all that the shepherd boy offered Me spontaneously
in his innocent and unpolished words as they may
appear to you, but I am highly displeased with you
for having driven him from his communing with
Me. I am not affected by words alone, for whatever they be, they do not in any way sanctify Me
but purify the heart of him who utters them. I see
not to the glossy words but to the heart and the
inner sincerity that lies therein behind the words,
for it is from the abundance of heart that a man
speaks, no matter in what broken and uncouth
words he may give expression to his feelings. O
Moses! there is a world of difference between the
learned, entangled in the etiquette of polished
speech, and the love-stricken hearts that give vent
to what is within them, the withered souls in the
waste-land of the heart, lost to all sense of decency
and decorum as you would call it. Don't you know
that even the Government does not impose any
land revenue on a land that is *banjar* or a waste.
A martyr in God needs thy care and attention. The
religion of love is quite different from the religion
of set formalism and ritual and for the lovers there
is no religion higher than that of God Himself. A
jewel remains a jewel even if it has no hallmark
on it.

When Moses heard these words, he felt terrified and went to the jungle, found out the shepherd boy and said, "I have brought for you happy tidings. God has accepted all your prayer and your seemingly heretic words are as good as those of a devout and your devotion is the light of your body. Whatever comes to you from within, utter without any fear." The boy replied smilingly, "O Moses, I have now far transcended all the barriers of the flesh. Your rebuke was enough to bring in me a great change. Now I know the Great One and my condition is that which no words can portray."

15. Time for Prayer

PRAYER needs no specific time nor any particular hour. In fact, one can pray without ceasing. It is an ebullition of spirit and like a volcano may burst at any moment. Prayer should, however, be offered regularly at any time during the day or night. Early morning hours and evening twilight hours are, of course, very congenial and most suitable.

> At the ambrosial hour of the early dawn,
> Be ye in communion with the Divine Word,
> And meditate on His glory.[53]

GURU NANAK

Most of us search for a time for prayer and unfortunately are so busy that in the end we find no time at all. A prayer does not need any philosophic dissertation or elaborate arrangement. One has just in loving faith to express his inner urge in the simplest words possible.

A true prayer needs no particular time and place. We have to sit quietly in the temple of the body, at the seat of the soul, and to gaze in between the eyebrows and mentally repeat whatever charged words have been given to us by the Master. That is more than enough of a prayer. But the trouble with us is that we do not know how to pray. We may in a case like this simply ask, "O Lord! teach us how to pray." In this respect, we can be guided by the specimen prayers given by the various Masters.

16. Occasion for Prayer

WE GENERALLY pray when we are in distress and trouble, but when we escape therefrom we begin thinking that we wrought liberation by our own efforts and thereafter do not feel the need for prayer. We must guard against such serious pitfalls. Prayer in fact is needed at every step. When in difficulty we must pray to escape therefrom. In distress, when all else fails, the thought of the Omnipotent Father gives solace to the mind. When success be in sight, then pray that you may not get elated and puffed up and ask for God's Grace and bounty for without these we can never succeed. After the fulfillment of our desires or riddance from difficulties, we must render thanks to the Almighty for His favors. When God is the loving Father and we cannot do without Him at all, prayer must become a part of our very being.

17. *Prayer and Sin*

A MERE confession of sins and shortcomings in prayer does not avail anything. If we think that by mere confession our sins can be washed off and we can once again indulge in them freely we are wrong. Such an attitude, far from being a saving force, keeps us perpetually down in sins. Redemption is the gift that comes either from God or the Godman who specifically comes for the benefit of sinners. Our job is just to understand his commandments and to keep them scrupulously, leaving the rest to him.

> *How may one know the Truth and break*
> *through the cloud of falsehood?*
> *There is a Way, O Nanak: To make His Will*
> *our own,*
> *His Will which is already wrought in our*
> *existence.*[54]
>
> GURU NANAK

Every action has a reaction. Every act of omission or commission has an appropriate penalty. We cannot escape from sin as long as we consider ourselves as born of the flesh, for flesh is the root cause of all evils in the world. Until a spirit learns to leave the sensual plane at will, enjoyments and distractions do thrive like a bay tree.

> *Too much indulgence means distress,*
> *Enjoyments lead ultimately to disease.*

Pleasures cannot chase away pain,
Without His acceptance one wanders in the
wilderness.[55]

GURU NANAK

God is all love. To think that it is because of our forgiveness that He forgives us for trespasses, or else He
would not do so, is to misunderstand Him and make
a misuse of prayers as means for doing more wrongs.

The man of God, on the other hand, has a twofold
plan of Dispensation. While granting forgiveness for
faults on the one hand he remonstrates severely against
repetition. "Thus far and no further," is his admonition.
"Go and sin no more," was a familiar phrase with
Christ when he used to forgive the sinners. In this way
he works out his purificatory process and the spirit is
chiseled into a shape and form that may be acceptable
to God.

Prayer *per se* cannot alter His Law of Dispensation
nor help to reach Him. It is only the loving and intense
longing for God and strict obedience to the commandments of the Godman that make a prayer a means leading Godward. Love, and not loud prayers, is the corner-
stone of God's Law of Redemption.

If we lovingly depend upon the strong arm of the
Godman, his Grace gushes out spontaneously from the
fountain of love in him. "Reciprocity in love" is pro-
verbial indeed, and there is no limit to his saving Grace.
Even the penalty that he imposes is tinted with rays of
love, with no trace of rancor in it.

18. Prayers for Others

SINCE all souls are of the same essence as of God and are correlated with each other, one may as well pray for the benefit of others. High souls always pray for the good of the entire humanity. They are not content with the greatest good for the greatest number as is commonly sought by the leaders of society. Their prayers generally end with the words—"O God, do good unto all."

The Muslims first pray for the *Momins* (their brethren in faith), and thereafter for all the rest. The Buddhists likewise pray for all. Christ even suggested prayer for one's enemies. Amongst the Hindus it is a common practice to close their prayers with a few charitable words for all living creatures great and small. Some people offer prayers for the ills of the entire humanity and still others make use of it in the case of individual ailments. Telepathy has now conclusively proved how heartstrings between individuals play in unison, irrespective of distance between the two. There is a tremendous power in thought vibrations and their range is unlimited. Is not the coming into being of the countless universes and their dissolution the result of some thought-force, if we may be permitted to use the phrase as indicative of God's Will, no matter what we may call it—*Kalma,* Word, *Hukam,* or *Bhana.* Thus the sympathetic chords between the Master and the disciples carry silent messages of love to and fro between them with a force that is unimaginable. This wonderful relationship one can establish with God. By being in tune with the Infinite one can by force of thought do a lot of good to others, as at bottom all are embedded in the same soil, the Divine ground.

19. Acceptance of Prayers

IT IS a common experience that most of our prayers get no response. The reason for this is not hard to find. We have not yet learnt the Will of God and how that Will works entirely for our benefit. In our ignorance we very often pray for things that in the long run are likely to do more harm than good, and no wonder that the loving Father in His boundless compassion for us does not accept such prayers and they bear no fruit, or else we would never be able to escape from sensual enjoyments.

> *Ye ask and receive not, because ye ask amiss*
> *that ye may consume it upon your lusts.*

Again:

> *We ignorant of ourselves,*
> *Beg often our own harms, which the wise*
> *   powers*
> *Deny us for our good; so find we profit*
> *By losing of our prayers.*
> > SHAKESPEARE

George Meredith tells us to remember,

> *That he who rises from prayer a better man,*
> *his prayer alone is answered.*

Again, we generally pray to God for miracles and no wonder such prayers are not granted.

Whatever a man prays for, he prays for a miracle.

Every prayer reduces itself to this: "Great God, grant that twice two be not four."

TURGENIEV

All the time we are living a sensual life and have not yet known that there is another side of the picture as well —life beyond the senses. Most of our prayers are, therefore, of a temporal nature and if they were granted without any exception we would naturally sink lower and lower in the scale of moral values and our sins increase more and more day by day, and there would hardly be a chance to get out of these prison-houses of the world and of the body and bodily enjoyments, with the result that we would forever remain an exile from the Kingdom of God—a Lost Province—with no hope for reunion.

When a disciple remembers the Master, he experiences within him a soothing influence and a sort of Divine intoxication. This is known as telepathy or sympathetic communication from heart to heart from a distance. In the same way we can, by tuning our attention with the Infinite, draw upon the great reservoir of God-Power and utilize that for the beneficent good of others. For this purpose one has to unite his self in the Divine ground wherein all are embedded and from there pass on the heavenly influence to the individual or society desired to be benefited. In this attitude one has not to place the desires of others before the Creator, but has simply to invoke His loving pleasure and await His Grace to work out the desired result.

> If Radio's slim fingers can pluck a melody
> From night, and toss it over a continent or sea,
> Why should mortals wonder if God hears
>   prayer.
>
> ETHIL ROMING FULLER

But man is just a part of the creation and each individual but an infinitesimal speck therein. Gifted as we are with a limited vision, we do not know and understand that Grand Plan, that "Mighty Maze" as Alexander Pope, the Laureate of peace, puts it: it is indeed too much for "presumptuous man . . . so weak, so little and so blind," a tiny part in the vast machinery of His creation. Again the great poet tells us:

> Heaven from all creatures hides the book of
>   fate.
> All but the page prescribed, their present
>   state . . .
> All Nature is but art, unknown to thee;
> All chance, direction, which thou canst not see;
> All discord, harmony not understood;
> All partial evil, universal good.
> And, spite of pride, in erring reason's spite,
> The Truth is clear, "Whatever is, is right" . . .
> Know then thyself, presume not God to scan,
> The proper study of mankind is Man,
> Chaos of Thought and Passion all confused . . .

Great Lord of all things, yet a prey to all,
Sole Judge of Truth, in endless Error hurled.

Each one, therefore, from his narrow angle of vision
prays for a thing and knows not how it will fit in the
Cosmic Order. In the hot and sultry months, for example, people living in towns pray for a refreshing shower,
while in the rural areas peasants at the same time ask
for more sunshine and heat for ripening their corn.

Man looks not beyond his nose. He does not even
know what is good for him. Often he asks for things
which, when granted, become a veritable source of nuis-
ance to him, and with much regret he has to retrace his
steps. The story of the "Golden Touch" is significant in
this connection. King Midas after much longing and
prayer got the boon of converting everything he touched
into gold. After a few moments of happiness he realized
his mistake. The food he put into his mouth turned into
a lump of gold. The water as it touched his lips solidi-
fied into gold. His only daughter as she came running
and embraced him became a statue of gold. As he went
to the soft bed he found himself on hard metallic cush-
ions.

God or Godman knows best. Our past and future are
like an open book to Him. He would never grant such
prayers as are ultimately baneful to us. How can the
loving Father give to a child that which might prove a
poison to him? A Persian poet says:

My God is more anxious than myself to fulfill
my needs,

*All my endeavors in this behalf are but tortuous
deeds.*

One should pray to God for such gifts as He may
consider beneficial.

*O God, I know not what is good for me, for
I am immersed head and ears in the maze
of the world.*[56]

RAVIDAS

Khwaja Nizami prayeth:

*O God! Thou alone art my well-wisher. Show
me the way whereby I may win Thy Grace
and attain salvation.*

In the holy Koran also it is stated that people ought to
pray for that which may be useful both in this world
and in the next.

20. Need for Prayer

WE CANNOT win God either by flattery or by vain
repetitions, nor does He stand to gain or lose
anything whether we offer prayers or not. Compassionate
as He is, His Grace is always at work in each and all
alike for we cannot live without It. We can, however,
attract that Grace to our advantage by becoming a fit
receptacle for It. Humility and faith purify the mind
and make it a fit instrument for God's Grace. These two
aids help in inverting the lotus of the mind which at
present is attuned with the senses. Unless we are able to
turn its direction upward, God's Grace cannot flow
directly into it. Prayers, humble and sincere, help in

establishing a harmony between man's mind and God's Grace. He needs no forensic arguments and legal acumen in defense of our deeds and needs. All that is required is a pure and loving heart attuned to His Grace and the latter is automatically attracted to it.

God is all Love, and we cannot ask Him to be more loving. He is Omniscient, and we cannot by loud and strong prayers make Him any wiser. Perfection cannot be made more perfect by our protestations and prayers. We must learn to "stand and wait" as the classic poet Milton puts it, and His Grace shall of its own be attracted and flood our very being.

> . . . *God doth not need*
> *Either man's work or His own gifts; who best*
> *Bear His mild yoke, they serve Him best; His*
> *state*
> *Is kingly, thousands at His bidding speed*
> *And post o'er land and ocean without rest:*
> *They also serve, who only stand and wait.*

JOHN MILTON

God is an unchangeable permanence and eternally the same:

> *He was when there was nothing;*
> *He was before all ages began;*
> *He existeth now, O Nanak,*
> *And shall exist forevermore.*[57]

GURU NANAK

> *Eternity is ever in love with the products of*
> *time.*

W. B. YEATS

The way to God's Grace lies not in striving and crying.
It is enough for man to wait silently as a receptacle for
Divine breath which bloweth where it listeth. It is merely
by waiting and trusting that one arrives at the Ultimate
Truth, which cannot be apprehended at all except as
it is focused upon the soul of man. Here lies the advantage of prayer which molds a correct attitude for approach to the Divine Will.

Wheresoever I turn my face, Thou art there,
Why should I pray to anyone else, when I see
Thou art there to listen to my prayer, O Lord.[58]

GURU ARJAN

Man's only duty is to be ever grateful to God for His
innumerable gifts and blessings. On the contrary, we
become so infatuated by them that we not only lose
Him but lose our own self also in the plenitude of His
bounties and more often than not are carried off our
feet by the whirlwind of desires.

We get attached to the gifts, forgetting the
bountiful Lord.
For we have forgotten that we have to die
some day.[59]

GURU ARJAN

21. The Advantages of Prayer

PRAYER is the essence of spirituality. It affords a wonderful recreation to the body, mind and soul. It
brings in complete satisfaction and satiation which
nothing else can give. The peace which comes with

prayer is of a unique nature, quite unimaginable. A kind of serenity descends upon the subliminal self within.

Prayer has in it a great dynamic force. It strengthens and befits a person to face and fight the battle of life fearlessly and successfully. It is in fact the only panacea for all types of ills: *Adhi Bhutak* (diseases and ailments), *Adhi Devak* (accidents over which man has no control), *Adhi Atmic* (evil propensities of the mind), and above all brings in inner peace and satiety. It buckles a person with courage and fortitude and brings about a complete reorientation.

Prayer is the key that unlocks the Kingdom of Heaven. It pulls up the sluice gates and releases from within immense power and resourcefulness.

> *Where all human efforts fail, there prayer succeeds.*

Lord Tennyson tells us,

> *. . . More things are wrought by prayer than this world dreams of.*

Even if prayer may seem to fail to avert calamity, yet it has the power to take the sting out of it. With an inner transformation there comes a change in the angle of vision, which greatly affects the outlook on life. Everything puts on a new mantle of color superbly Divine.

Last but not least, prayer opens our eyes to Reality and enables us to see things in their true perspective. It gives new values to life and gradually transports an individual into a New World and initiates him into a

New Order. With a life of prayer a person eventually rises into cosmic awareness and sees the hidden hand of God working out His will and His purpose which otherwise remain a sealed book too subtle for the average man to pierce through and peep into. The more this inner contact is established, the more Godhead is imbibed by the spirit. Only when a complete identification comes about does one become a conscious co-worker with Him.

22. Gradations in Prayer

IN THE course of time an aspirant begins to feel more and more the need for spiritual uplift than for mere physical comforts. In *Brihadaranyaka Upanishad* we have this prayer:

> *From the unreal lead me to the real, from darkness lead me to light and from death lead me to immortality.*

As soon as an aspirant begins to have inner experience, all worldly enjoyments lose their charm. Having had an experience, howsoever little, of the Unchangeable Permanence, he now finds no pleasure in the ever-changing objects of the world, subject as they are to gradual decay, disintegration and ultimate dissolution. He asks no more for physical comforts.

> *What shall I pray for, when nothing is permanent.*[60]
>
> KABIR

The whole world is slavishly mad, following the Epi-

curean principle "Eat, drink and be merry." None has
time to think of God and the inner Self. But nothing
in the world holds any attraction for a true aspirant.
He makes best use of whatever comes in his way and
works but to satisfy the bare needs of his body, and
spends the rest of his time in *Sadhna* (spiritual disci-
pline) so as to derive the greatest benefit for his soul.

> *For times without number have I drunk life to*
> *   the lees.*
> *Without Thy Saving Grace, O Lord! Nanak*
> *   hath no release.*[61]
>
>   GURU ARJAN

Hereafter the aspirant lives just for the manifestation
of God-head within himself and to sing the glory of His
name.

> *Let the lotus feet of the Master rest in the*
> *   heart,*
> *Let the tongue repeat His Holy Word,*
> *To live a life of constant remembrance nurture*
> *   ye this living temple of the Lord.*[62]
>
>   GURU ARJAN

While on this Path the pilgrim traveler realizes his
ignorance, and knowing his incapacity extends to God
his hands in prayer:

> *O Lord! make me swim safely to the other*
> *   shore,*
> *I know not swimming, extend to me Thy hand*
> *   of help.*[63]
>
>   NAMDEV

As his angle of vision changes, so does the nature of his prayer. At first a person prays for the fulfillment of his physical needs; but when one starts on the spiritual Path he prays for the removal of such obstacles as come in his way, e.g., sense-turmoil, mental chattering, ingrained karmic impressions.

This period is most critical in the life of a *sadhak*. Until actual self-realization he is in a state of perpetual restlessness, tossing back and forth. He belongs wholly neither to the world nor to God. While in the eyes of worldly people he is a man of piety, yet in the heart of his heart he knows he is full of iniquities.

> *Farid the sinful is still robed in black,*
> *Though the people address him as Darvesh.*
>
> FARID SAHIB

In this state of uncertainty the *sadhak* at times tries to snap away and escape from the struggle; but after a time the inner urge once again comes upon him and he takes courage and starts Godward.

> *Should a traveler while traveling fall down,*
> *There is nothing to wonder and cavil at.*
> *O Kabir! one who sits and starts not on the journey,*
> *Has an immeasurable distance yet to traverse.*

But until a person is able to subdue his senses and sensory organs and rid the mind of oscillations, the kindly Light of God does not dawn upon him.

> *Blessed are the pure in heart, for they shall see God.*[64]

If thine eye be single, thy whole body shall be full of light.[65]

CHRIST

He who controls his ten organs,
Heaven's Light dawns within him.[66]

GURU ARJAN

The wiles of the mind are both very subtle and risky. It often lies in ambush and makes its inroads when least expected. The ingrained evil propensities though invisible are very strong, and time and again they come to the surface to deliver blows which often prove fatal. The coil strikes out like lightning, with such sharp and sudden twists and turns that man by himself is helpless in its clutches. Here comes the need for the long and strong arm of the Master, which stretches forth with equal agility to his rescue:

Subdue the mind with the Power of the Master.

SWAMI SHIV DAYAL SINGH

Mind cannot come to rest unless it is over-shadowed by the power of the Master.

MAULANA RUMI

The sleeping mind comes to its own
By constant thought of the Master.[67]

GURU RAM DAS

23. What to Ask from God

A LADY on marriage entrusts her all to her husband and gladly accepts the new mode of life whatever it be. Now nothing else appeals to her but him. It is for the husband now to provide all her needs and to look after her comforts.

> *Render unto Him all that belongs to Him,*
> *And make His Will thine own.*
> *In return He showers His blessings manifold,*
> *O Nanak! He is ever so merciful.*[68]

> *He who has Him as his boon companion,*
> *He stands in need of naught.*[69]

GURU ARJAN

Once a certain king intended to go abroad. He inquired of his queens as to what gift each of them would like him to bring for them from the foreign lands. One of them asked for costly jewels, another for rich apparel and still another for cosmetics. Some asked for fineries and others for delicacies, etc. The youngest of them, who loved the king most, requested his early return so that she would not have to languish long in his absence. The king on his return sent the various gifts to his other queens and himself went to the palace of the youngest and was highly pleased that there was someone who loved him the most, much more than his riches and wealth. The queen too thanked God for her good fortune that her husband was with her and that she needed nothing else. The rest of the queens, though each one of them had got what she wanted, had not the good fortune to claim their husband's attention. All their riches and gifts availed them not without their beloved.

In exactly the same way we, through shortsightedness, ask from God or Godman for trinkets of no consequence and not Him and His Saving Grace, and like the different queens in the parable, suffer most the pangs of separation. All the riches of the world fail to give the least satisfaction. On the contrary, these things distract us from the Truth and make us more miserable. If we could but win His Grace we would then be in want no more. All His riches come to us automatically, without asking. Even if they are denied for one reason or another, it matters not, for without Him and His love they are dirty trash.

> All riches and fineries befit him who has won
> Him,
> And even without them, what care if he were
> to live in poverty.[70]

GURU ARJAN

Our most elementary needs are of the body—to wit, food, clothing and shelter. For these things we strive hard, working madly and restlessly from morn till night. We sacrifice our very self to procure these comforts— if any comfort they provide. Do we not realize that when a child comes into the world his life plan is sketched out beforehand? Without this nobody would be here at all. With destiny all shaped, the mould is cast and the spirit enters therein, ready to take his life's journey in the world.

> With a predestined plan one comes into the
> world,
> O Tulsi! with all this, the mind does not
> accept it.

Dame Nature now gets ready for the royal reception of the Prince of the Universe, providing milk in the mother's breast, shelter in the mother's lap, and an army of attendants to attend to his minutest needs. The Powers of Nature mobilize all their forces to claim the prince-child as their own. But as the child grows and develops into adolescence and begins to feel the life-impulse surging in him, the world, as a foster mother, claims him as her own and he fondly clings to her and her gifts forgetting his native and prenatal home in heaven.

> *Heaven lies about us in our infancy,*
> *Shades of the prison-house begin to close upon*
>   *the growing boy.*
> *Earth fills her lap with pleasures of her own;*
> *Yearning she hath in her own natural kind,*
> *And even with something of a mother's mind,*
>   *and no unworthy aim,*
> *The homely nurse doth all she can,*
> *To make her foster child, her inmate Man,*
>   *forget the glories he hath known,*
> *And that imperial palace whence he came.*
>
> **WORDSWORTH**

Again, all the gifts of the world are purely ephemeral. They are always in an unstable and changing state. Nothing is permanent. Everything is subject to decay and dissolution.

> *Momentarily things appear and then recede*
>   *back into the Fullness,*
> *In the twinkling of an eye the world itself sinks*
>   *into the great deep.*[71]
>
> **KABIR**

Midst the ever-changing phenomena of the world, there is but one unchangeable permanence and that is God and God-in-action (the Holy Spirit, *Kalma, Naam* or Word), responsible for the creation, sustenance and dissolution of countless universes. Why then should we not long for, ask for and pray for that imperishable life principle, so that we too may have "Life Everlasting" and come to our eternal heritage, the everlasting Godhood which is our birthright.

> *Listen ye to the call of the hollow man, manifest Thyself, O Lord,*
> *Nanak has humbly reached Thy door, through the Grace of Thy devotee.*[72]

GURU ARJAN

Our native home is in *Sach Khand.* Ages upon ages have gone by since we parted from the Father and we are still in exile in this world.

> *The soul that rises with us, our life's Star,*
> *Hath had elsewhere its setting,*
> *And cometh from afar.*

WORDSWORTH

We must then yearn for a reunion with the Beloved, separated as we are from Him for myriads of ages.

> *For ages upon ages have we been separated,*
> *Unite us unto Thee, O Lord, through sheer compassion if Thou wilt.*
> *We have wandered high and low in all the points of the compass,*

*Now keep us O Thou under the shadow of
Thy holy wings.*[73]

GURU ARJAN

*In countless births have I wandered away and
away from Thee,
This (human) birth I have dedicated to Thee
and staked on Thee,
Ravidas now lives in hope to meet Thee once
again.*[74]

RAVIDAS

Guru Amar Das, therefore, prayeth:

*Through innumerable gyres have I gone with-
out rest,
In Thy mercy, O Merciful! grant me the boon
of Thy manifestation.*[75]

Guru Arjan prayeth:

*Many a birth I had in various species,
Every time I had to undergo many sufferings.
Through Thy Grace I have now a human
birth,
This then is the time to manifest Thyself unto
me, O Lord.*[76]

*Lift me O Lord! I have fallen at Thy door,
Accept me in compassion, tired as I am of my
wanderings.
Savior of Thy devotees, save the sinners as well,
I know none besides Thee to offer my prayers,
O ferry me safely across the ocean of living
matter.*[77]

The soul pines in the separation of her Lord. Even if
she is not worthy of the Lord, she prays for union with
Him.

All are blessed in the love of their Lord,
But I alone am the unfortunate one.
So filled with spots through and through,
My consort does not like even to see my face.[78]

GURU AMAR DAS

Meritless as I am, I intensely pray for my
turn, O Nanak,
All the spouses had Thee in abundance, spare
a night for me as well.[79]

All the maidens have gone with their spouses,
Where should I, the unfortunate, turn my face?
With my parents I was the light of their eyes,
But woe unto me that my Lord looks not at
me.[80]

GURU AMAR DAS

Kill me if Thou wilt but turn not away,
Hug me to Thy bosom, listen ye to my prayer,
Just look this way and earn my gratitude,
Why kill me by turning Thy face away.[81]

KABIR

Thirsty as I am for Thy sight,
My mind calls for Thee in agony,
I pray to Thee O Formless! and crave for Thy
mercy.[82]

Life is worth living with Thee before me.
Be merciful, O sweet Beloved,
And drive away all doubts and delusions.[83]

I earnestly beseech and pray for just one thing,
I make a sacrifice of all my wealth and posses-
sions for a union with Thee.[84]

GURU ARJAN

What may I ask for and repeat unto Thee
except
That I hunger and thirst for Thy sight;
It is through the Word of the Master that one
reaches Truth,
Nanak, therefore, prays for this alone.[85]

I have just one submission and listen ye to
that,
Certainly Thou art great, compassionate, and
immaculate.[86]

GURU NANAK

We never remember Thee and waste our life
in fruitless pursuits.
Nanak sayeth, O God, remember Thou the
pledge (of redemption), regardless of our
defaults.[87]

Thou art the abode of all virtues and Lord of
us all with no virtue in us,
No bondsman can praise Thee enough, when
he holds even his body and life from Thee.
Thou saved me from the hell-fires, I have
taken shelter at Thy feet,
Thou art the only stake of my life and honor,
I depend on naught else.[88]

Great is the Lord, boundless, infinite and
　ineffable,
O Nanak! He is the Savior of all who take
　refuge in Him.[89]

I pray to Thee, O Lord! of body, mind and
　soul,
O Nanak! it is His greatness else none knew
　me before.[90]

GURU ARJAN

Thou alone art the Doer of all things,
　To whom then should we offer prayers.[91]

GURU NANAK

Helpless are we and Merciful art Thou,
What can we, the sinners, say unto Thee.
In spite of our broken words of no meaning,
Accept us and grant us the gift of perfection.[92]

RAVIDAS

Thou art the woof and warp of my very exist-
　ence,
I, therefore, pray unto Thee alone.
I have no other place to turn to for worship,
I place all my comforts and discomforts before
　Thee.[93]

I cannot do justice to Thy greatness,
For I am an ignorant fool.
O Lord! redeem poor Nanak,
For he has taken shelter at Thy feet.[94]

GURU RAM DAS

Again, we have in the Sikh Scriptures:

> *We, the ignorant, insensate and devoid of all*
> *virtues, have taken refuge with Thee, O*
> *Primal Being,*
> *Through Thy Boundless Grace, O Lord! save*
> *us, in spite of all our shortcomings.*[95]

> *O God! have mercy and ferry us across,*
> *Save us with the help of Thy Melodious Song.*
> *We are bogged in the mire of infatuation,*
> *O extend to us Thy hand and pull us out.*[96]
>
> GURU RAM DAS

> *Look ye not on my merits and demerits,*
> *But forgive me my faults, O Merciful.*
> *How can the clay toy be washed clean?*
> *That indeed is the fate of all human beings.*[97]

> *O Lord! be Thou compassionate on the*
> *orphan at Thy door,*
> *Sustain him in the blind well of the body,*
> *For he is imbecile both in mind and intellect.*[98]

> *We are the great defaulters and sinners with a*
> *galaxy of thefts to boot,*
> *Now Nanak is at Thy feet, O Lord! save him*
> *as Thou wilt.*[99]
>
> GURU ARJAN

> *O Savior and Sustainer Peerless, listen ye to*
> *me,*
> *O Nanak! the ignorant and the foolish never*
> *think of Him,*

*Nor do they know the pitch dark night in
which they live.*[100]

GURU NANAK

*I have no virtues of the body or of the mind,
and have come from afar,
I have neither riches nor beauty, save me the
homeless one.* [101]

*One who slips at every step cannot escape on
his own account,
O Nanak, He may forgive and pilot me across
in His Divine Mercy.*[102]

GURU ARJAN

*We commit blunders without number, and
know not their consequences,
O Lord! forgive us in Thy Grace for we are
inveterate sinners.*[103]

GURU AMAR DAS

*Like the great deep sea, we are full of faults,
With Thy Mercy and Saving Grace, Thou
canst save the millstones from sinking
down.*[104]

GURU NANAK

The whole world is in the throes of death pangs. God
alone can save it, as He may with His limitless love.

*The entire world is being consumed in the
invisible flames of hellfire,
Save us all with Thy loving Grace in whatever
way it may be possible.*[105]

GURU AMAR DAS

O Lord! Thou art peerlessly deep and infin-
itely high and none reaches Thee,
We pray that we may not forget Thee, the
fountain of all comforts.[106]

GURU ARJAN

O the Great Giver and perfect Master,
I ask of Thee but one gift, the gift of Hari.
Shower Thy blessings on Nanak,
O my oldest Friend, become manifest in me.[107]

GURU RAM DAS

Good and evil intentions are both in your control,
O Lord. We are but instruments and You are the motor-
power behind us. We only act and do as You actuate
us from behind.

All our thoughts and good intentions are in
Thy control,
Thou alone art the motor-power behind all our
actions,
O Nanak! He is the overruling power that
works as He Wills.[108]

GURU RAM DAS

We, *per se,* are incapable of rendering any service to
God, and cannot pride ourselves on our so-called service.
It is in the refulgence of God's Light that we live and
have our very being. When He withdraws the life current, we become helpless:

None can serve Thee nor feel elated at any-
thing.

*When the life currents are withdrawn, how
    helpless we become.*[109]

GURU AMAR DAS

We must ask for God from God, for all else means
inviting headache. The greatest gift from Him is that
of *Naam* or the Power of Godhead, which when granted
brings with it contentment and satisfaction.

*Except Thee all else is the source of trouble
    and misery,
Grant us the gift of Thy Word that brings in
    peace and satiation.*[110]

GURU ARJAN

Maulana Rumi prayeth in this wise:

*Ask from God nothing but God.
Except Him, all else is perishable.
Never ask God for a thing that must decay,
Ask not of God anything beside Himself.
Darken not thy mind with thoughts and cares
    that are chimerical.*

(*i*) *Ask for God*:

One may invoke help in crucial moments of his life,
from God or from a Godman, for He alone can rescue
him from such slippery moments.

*Full of the deadly sins and tormented by lusts
    of the flesh I cry,
Rescue me by Thy Grace, as best Thou may.
O Great and Compassionate One! I am at
    Thy mercy,*

With austerities and penances one cannot
  escape,
But with Thy glance of Grace, take Nanak
  out of the blind well.[111]

O Lord! save me,
I am incapable of doing anything,
In Thy mercy, grant me the gift of Naam.[112]

GURU ARJAN

I pray to the Guru, the beloved of God,
A filthy worm am I, O grant me the light of
  Naam.[113]

GURU RAM DAS

Mind can be controlled only by the *Dhun* of *Naam* or
the celestial strains of music, and it is for this that one
has to pray. No other type of yoga—*Jnana, Hatha,
Karma,* etc.— can be of any avail in this connection;
nor has anyone been able to escape from the clutches
of the mind with all his wits about him. One may tame
the wild mind only through the practice of *Sat-Shabd*
or *Naam* (the True Word) and one can have initiation
into this practice from some adept in the line. The
moment it comes into contact with *Naam,* the mind gets
docile and instead of being an arch-traitor as hitherto,
it turns into a positive ally and helps the spirit in its
onward march on the Spiritual Path.

O I have got the treasure of Hari Naam,
My mind now wanders not but is in eternal
  rest.[114]

GURU TEG BAHADUR

Listening to the Dhun, the mind gets stilled,
None of the myriad of ways can work this
*   miracle.*
The yogin practices yogic exercises,
The Jnani is immersed in Jnana.
The hermit tires himself out in lone solitude,
The anchorite does endless austerities.
Those who meditate on the mental patterns,
They too suffer from a great delusion.
Learning and knowledge are of not much avail,
For the wise in the end have to rue their
*   wisdom.*
The Pandit engages in the recitation of the
*   Vedas*
But all his sacred lore fails to take him any
*   nearer to God.*
No other means are of any consequence what-
*   ever,*
The only beneficial way is that of Shabd.
When a Master of the Sound Current appears
*   on the scene,*
The disciple too begins to feel the yearning of
*   the new birth.*
With the practice of the Surat Shabd Yoga,
The mind-stuff gradually sinks within itself
*   till nothing remains.*[115]

SWAMI SHIV DAYAL SINGH

When once this contact with Naam is established, the
Sadhak always feels the presence of the Higher Power
and the Power remains forever with him wherever he

may be—on the snowy mountain tops or in the burning desert sands. Reveling in the greatness of that Power he leaves all his cares to Him and becomes indifferent to everything around him. He cheerfully accepts whatever comes his way as coming from Him for his benefit alone. He consciously sees the Divine Will at work and smilingly surrenders himself to it with words of genuine gratitude on his lips. He has no longer any wishes and desires of his own except what may be of God. Now he works as a mere instrument moving like an automaton under the influence of that Power. He sees all creatures, high and low, just as tiny specks set in an orderly harmony in the immense Universe surrounding him. He now divines a procession which is orderly, an order which is harmonious, obeying a Will infinitely above him and yet infinitesimally careful of him. In this way is established a complete harmony between the soul of man and the soul of the Universe. At every step he cries forth, Let thy Will be done:

All creatures, the highest to the lowest, are at
Thy mercy, and Thou carest for them one
and all.
Whatever pleaseth Thee, that is best; Nanak
has no other wish but this.[116]

Whatever pleaseth Thee is good,
Thou art forevermore,
O Formless one.[117]

GURU NANAK

O Nanak! Great is the Power of Naam,
Let there be peace unto all, through Thy Will.

The pontifical blessings generally end with the words:
Urbi et Orbi (to the citizen and the world).

In the end there comes a stage when the *Sadhak* feels
no necessity even for prayer.

> *Sweet art Thy doings,*
> *Nanak desireth only Hari Naam.*[118]

> *In whatsoever state I am, that is a Heaven*
> *unto me.*[119]

GURU ARJAN

When God is the Knower of the secrets of all, there
hardly remains anything to be told Him. With the Lord
seated in each one of us and permeating our very being,
what need is there to pray and to whom?

> *Hari is the Indweller and knoweth all,*
> *To whom then art we to tell of us?*[120]

GURU ARJAN

> *What should the lowly urge for*
> *When God is seated within all?*[121]

GURU RAM DAS

Saints always live in this state. Being one with His Will
and conscious co-workers with Him, prayer of itself
becomes a heresy for them and savors of scepticism.
Nature's forces simply wait on them. However slight a
thought may arise, it must, like an immutable law,
prevail. God is ever with His devotee and looks after
him with more care and attention than any loving
mother would give her child.

Guru Arjan tells us:

> *He who asks from the Lord, whatever it be,*
>   *that is granted forthwith,*
> *O Nanak! the words of the devotee do come*
>   *true wherever he may be.*
> *For the sake of His devotee He runs far and*
>   *near,*
> *And stands ever by his side,*
> *Whatever the devotee asks of Him, that must*
>   *happen.*[122]

Kabir, describing the condition of his mind, tells us
that it has, like the water of Ganges, become so trans-
parent that even God has become enamored of him:

> *Kabir, thy mind is now as clear as the Ganges*
>   *water.*
> *Even God Himself restlessly follows thee shout-*
>   *ing, "Kabir, Kabir."*[123]

When all the desires of a devotee get automatically fulfilled, he naturally becomes desireless. The wish-yielding
treasure of *Naam*, becoming manifest within, takes care
of him at every step.

> *With the Lord God as a loving Father, the*
>   *child has no hunger for aught, for*
> *Thou art the treasure-house of Naam and he*
>   *gets whatever he wishes.*[124]

> *The prayers of the devotee cannot go in vain.*[125]
>
> GURU ARJAN

When the Great Donor is with the devotee, the devotee

has nothing to pray for; for he is one with Him and there is nothing besides whom he may address.

Guru Arjan draws a wonderful pen-picture of this state of perfect satiety:

> *Deathless is He and I have nothing to fear,*
> *He being Immortal, I have not to wail;*
> *He is not poor and I have no want,*
> *He being above sorrow and pain, I too have*
> *none;*
> *Besides Him there is no destroyer, He and I*
> *live eternally,*
> *When He is free, there is nothing to bind me,*
> *Both of us are above the stage of bondage;*
> *He being Immaculate, I too have no stain,*
> *He being within me, what taint can I have?*
> *He has nothing to think of and nothing is left*
> *for me to think,*
> *Neither of us has anything to gloss over;*
> *Desireless is He and I too desire nothing,*
> *He is spotlessly pure and so am I,*
> *I have no existence apart from Him, for He*
> *alone is:*
> *O Nanak! through the Master has this delusion*
> *disappeared:*
> *Having dipped in Him, we are dyed in one*
> *color.*[126]

(ii) *Ask for Guru* (*A competent Living Master*)

The Lord is overflowing in the Guru. "Being immanent in the Guru, He distributes the Word." The Guru is God personified. Pray to the Lord:

Oh Merciful Father, the Destroyer of our ills,
be kind and send us the Satguru. He is the
very support of our life. Through Him alone
we can attain to Thee.
Thou art Merciful and the Destroyer of all
our ills. Attend to our prayer. Please make us
search for the Satguru, through whom we
know Thee.[127]

O Lord, the very Soul of the Universe, grant
us faith in Naam (the Mystic Word), and
the benevolent and purifying company of
the true men.[128]

O Lord, allow us that Satguru, remembering
whom we shall be liberated. At his very
Darshan (a sight of him) the mind feels
exhilarated. We shall again and again lay
our very life at his lotus feet.[129]

GURU RAM DAS

Beg from the Lord and the Guru their Divine Vision,
complete self-surrender and the gift of *Naam*. Pray also
to be saved from the evil tendencies of the mind and the
senses. Being Omnipotent, He is capable of granting us
all these boons. Besides this, the seekers may pray for
the gift of happily resigning to His sweet Will. We have
no good qualities in us. Being ignorant and of low mental caliber, we are not well versed in religious cere-
monies, etc. Therefore, oh Beloved! have mercy on us.
Bestow on us the capacity to sing Thy praises and to
remain happy in whatever be Thy Will.

Virtueless, blind, ignorant and unlettered as
*   we are,*
We know not what is good for us or for
*   society,*
Be merciful, O Lord! that Nanak may sing of
*   Thee,*
And may ever rejoice in Thy Will and Pleas-
*   ure.*[130]

GURU RAM DAS

In addition to this, pray for the grant of devotion and
of *Naam*.

By repeatedly uttering Thy Naam, we are
*   freed from doubt and fear,*
Those who are absorbed in Thy sweet remem-
*   brance will be freed from the cycle of birth*
*   and death.*[131]

GURU ARJAN

We are humble mendicants at Thy door,
Be gracious enough to bless us with Thine
*   Amrit (Nectar) of the Word,*
Satguru is my Master Friend, please grant me
*   his contact.*[132]

GURU RAM DAS

Forgive me for my lack of good qualities and
*   make me your own, my Master,*
Thou art Infinite and Unknowable,
Graciously make known to me Thyself through
*   Shabd—the Mystic Word.*[133]

GURU AMAR DAS

*My Lord, the Creator, is the Ocean of all
    goodness,
Who can adequately praise Him?
Saints pray for the gift of the highest bliss of
    Naam.*[134]

GURU ARJAN

*We are but humble mendicants and beggars,
    Thou art the Protector of our honor,
Be kind and give us the alms of Thy Naam, so
    that we may remain always intoxicated in
    Thy love.*[135]

GURU AMAR DAS

*O Lord! take us under the shadow of Thy
    protecting wings,
We are unable to do anything on our own,
Graciously give us Thy Naam.*[136]

*O my Divine Friend, grant that I may every
    day make an effort to think only of Thee all
    the time,
O give me a contact with Shabd—the Bread
    of life.*[137]

*The company of Saints dyes us with His Naam
    and all our desires are fulfilled,
Nanak prays for Thy Mercy and Thy Grace
    and that we may remain absorbed in the
    sweet memory of Thy lotus feet.*[138]

GURU ARJAN

O Rama! make us the servant of Thy Servants.

Grant us the boon to bask in the light of Saints
so long as the breath of our life lasts.[139]

GURU RAM DAS

O Merciful Lord! Graciously grant us the
radiant dust from the feet of Saints.[140]

GURU AMAR DAS

24. Guru Is the Greatest Gift of God

THE truest riches and the greatest gift of God is the
Godman, the person who, having realized himself,
is established in his Godhead. He is in a sense a polarized
God or pole from which God manifests Himself amongst
His people. Limitless and Infinite as God is, He is
beyond comprehension by finite powers of perception.
He can, however, be apprehended in the Master some-
what as a vast sea can be apprehended at the beach
with bathing *ghats,* where sea waters gently flow in so
bathers can have a safe dip.

As like attracts like, man must of necessity have man
as his teacher, for no one else can teach him. The way to
God, therefore, lies through man. Some Godman alone
can tell us of the "Way out" from the world and a
"Way in" into the Kingdom of God, now a Lost Province to mankind in general. The fall of man was brought
about by man and the regeneration of man too is to be
brought about by man. But there is a world of difference
between man and man—the latter being God-in-man.

Surely the Lord God will do nothing, but He

*revealeth His secrets unto His servants the
Prophets.*[141]

AMOS

All scripture is given by inspiration of God.[142]

ST. PAUL

*The Word became flesh and dwelt amongst
us.*[143]

ST. JOHN

Guru is God personified, for God speaks through the
Guru.

*Poor Nanak speaks whenever He desires him
to do so.*

GURU NANAK

*The words of the Master are the words of
Allah, though seemingly uttered by Abdul-
lah (the Servant of God).*

MAULANA RUMI

*I speak not of myself; but the Father that
dwelleth in me, He doeth the works.*[144]

CHRIST

The greatest prayer a person can therefore offer to God
is that He may, in His unbounded mercy, establish his
contact with His prophets who may lead him Godward.
The Godman or the Prophet shows him the Way—the
Grand Trunk Road that leads to God. It is nothing but
the Sound Current or Sound Principle differently called
by different sages: the Word or the Holy Spirit by the
Christians, *Kalma, Bang-e-Asmani* or *Nida-e-Arshi* by
the Mohammedans, *Udgit, Akash Bani, Naad* or *Sruti*

by the Hindus, and *Shabd* or *Naam* by the Sikhs. Zoroaster calls it *Sraosha* and the Theosophists "the Voice of
the Silence." Christ speaks of it as "The Voice of the
Son of God." God overflows in the Guru and unites
man with the Word to reach back to his True Home.

> *When the dead shall hear the Voice of the Son*
> *of God; and they that hear shall live.*[145]
>
> CHRIST

This Sound Current then is the means to salvation. It is
the Master Key that unlocks the Kingdom of Heaven.
It bestows life eternal on man and restores him once
again to the Garden of Eden from which he was driven
away by disobedience to God. What greater boon can
a man seek from God but restoration to the Kingdom
lost by him. It marks the end of his long exile through
countless centuries as He hails back the lost sheep to His
fold. The Master is the kind Shepherd who, out of compassion, does all this for erring humanity. Such high
souls hold a commission from the Most High.

> *I am come in my Father's name.*[146]
>
> *No man can come to me, except the Father*
> *which hath sent me draw him: and I will*
> *raise him up at the last day.*[147]
>
> CHRIST

We have similar references in the Sikh Scriptures as well.

> *Kabir knows the secrets of God and brings His*
> *message to mankind.*
>
> KABIR

> *He who sent thee into the world, He calls thee*

back again and wistfully awaits thy home-
coming.

GURU ARJAN

Herein lies the greatness of Master-souls. They effect a
reunion between man and God. The long-drawn period
of separation comes to an end and the lost child is
restored once again to the Father. It marks the Grand
Homecoming through endless trials and tribulations. The
Saving Grace of God is stirred by the Godman and the
purpose of life is fulfilled. Henceforth the Son and the
Father are not only reconciled but become one.

From the great deep to the great deep he goes.

TENNYSON

No longer is he an exile in the world but an inheritor
of the Kingdom of God, established once more in his
native Godhead.

This is the true fulfillment of the covenant between
God and man, and the true resurrection or rising from
the dead as vouchsafed by the Son of God to man. This
is the fulfillment of God's Law and the purpose of human
birth.

This is the fundamental Law of God: that no
one can reach Him except through Satguru
(the Master-soul).[148]

GURU RAM DAS

Again:

God clothed Himself in vile man's flesh, that so
He might be weak enough to suffer woe.

JOHN DONNE

Therefore, always pray God to bring us in contact with
a Godman—the Master.

25. What One Should Ask from the Godman

THE Master is the mouthpiece of God. He is the Pole
at which God manifests His Godhood. He is the
bathing *ghat* or beach where a person can safely enter
into the sea for a dip. He is like a switch, which has in
it the concentrated energy of the powerhouse. The Son
and the Father are one and administer the same Law.
"I and my Father are one," says Christ. Clothed in
Heavenly Light, He radiates Light into the world.

> *I am the light of the world, and he that fol-*
> *loweth me, shall not walk in darkness but*
> *shall have the light of life.*[149]
>
> CHRIST

God or a Godman is the Treasure House of *Naam*.
Naam is God's Master-instrument with which He created
the Universe and with which He is sustaining it. The
moment He withdraws this power of His, the result is
disintegration, dissolution and death.

Saint John calls It "Word:"

> *In the beginning was the Word, and the Word*
> *was with God and the Word was God. The*
> *same was in the beginning with God. All*
> *things were made by Him; and without Him*
> *was not anything made that was made. In*
> *Him was life; and the life was the light of*

*man. And the light shineth in darkness and
the darkness comprehendeth it not.*[150]

A prophet, a saint, an apostle is truly the repository of
God's Power. He is the veritable abode of God Himself:

*God comes into the world in the garb of a
Sadh (saint).*[151]

GURU ARJAN

Whoever then has a longing for God must hasten to a
true Saint and seek God from Him. Nothing but the
Saving Grace of the Master can work a true transformation in the worldly-wise man, fully identified as he is
with the sensual plane.

*I think of Thee and lovingly long for Thee,
I pray to the saints to manifest Thee in me.*[152]
*I pray to the sadhs for I hear God is of His
devotees,
Nanak has an intense longing for Him, O!
have mercy.*[153]

GURU ARJAN

*Separate for ages, unite now O Lord,
This is the greatest desire of my heart.
Hear my prayers through the Master,
Nanak has no other wish but this.*[154]

GURU RAM DAS

*I pray to the saints for union,
That is what Nanak asks for.*[155]

GURU ARJAN

*The souls that have realized the Lord, I shall
    inquire of them,
In all humility, I shall supplicate to know the
    Way to Him.*[156]

GURU NANAK

*Saints are the representatives of God, and to
    them we pray,
We are but filthy worms, O Satguru, grant us
    the light of Naam.*[157]

GURU RAM DAS

Bhai Gurdas has given us a beautiful specimen of prayer
for the Sikhs:

*I am a depraved sinner and a heretic,
A thief, a gambler and a housebreaker,
A thug that lives on illicit gains,
A constant prey to all kinds of lusts,
A slave to the five passions, viz., lust, anger,
    greed, attachment and egoism,
A betrayer, an ungrateful wretch, abhorred by
    all.
O ye, with all these faults, and still more,
Remember the Satguru for He is compas-
    sionate indeed.*[158]

Once this relationship of Master and disciple is established, the latter becomes fully dependent upon him. The
acceptance of the disciple by the Master means acceptance of the entire responsibility of his Karmic debt or
burden, including *Prarabdh* (fate or destiny), *Kriyaman*

(actions or deeds performed from day to day), and *Sanchit* Karmas (the storehouse of unfructified karmic impressions). Like an official liquidator, it is now his job to liquidate the debts of the disciple, wind them up and free him from them so as to put him on his feet again for the second birth leading to the life of the spirit.

> *We are now of the Master, a bond-slave unto Him,*
> *O Nanak! with the relationship of Master and servant, save us now.*[159]
>
> GURU RAM DAS

> *I long for an eternal friend,*
> *Ever true, from end to end.*[160]
>
> GURU ARJAN

> *I pray to the Satguru to lead me to the Friend,*
> *By meeting whom, peace descends and death vanishes.*[161]
>
> GURU NANAK

> *O Master! may I live by beholding Thee,*
> *And my life's aim be fulfilled.*
> *O fulfill my prayers that I may live by Thy Word,*
> *May I ever abide under Thy protection,*
> *Whose value only the blessed few may know,*
> *And that too only through the Master's Grace.*
> *Grant this boon, O my Beloved,*
> *That Thou may ever dwell in my mind.*
> *Nanak has but one wish alone,*

That he may never forget the fountainhead of
all virtues.[162]

Everything is in Thy Controlling Power, O
Destroyer of fear,
So saith Nanak, save the ignorant, O Merciful
One.[163]

GURU ARJAN

Seeing that the whole world is being consumed
in invisible flames of fire, I come to Thy feet,
I pray, O perfect Master, save us as Thou
wilt.[164]

GURU AMAR DAS

APPENDIX

Prayers

Miscellaneous and Brief Specimens

I T WILL *not be out of place to give below some specimen prayers for the benefit of the readers, with a few
introductory remarks in this behalf.*

*Man is an ensouled body, or in other words soul plus
body; and of the two, soul is the more precious because
it is the active and live-principle that enlivens the body.
In fact, body has no value apart from the soul.*

*The great souls or Mahatmas are of varied types.
There are Mahatmas who ask of God such necessities of
life as may keep their body and soul together, so that
after satisfying their physical needs they may spend their
time in meditation on God. Jesus in his prayer asked for
"daily bread" to satisfy Nature's foremost need—"Give
us this day our daily bread." Such souls regard everything as of God and ask Him for the fulfillment of
their primary needs from day to day and then engage
in uninterrupted devotion for the rest of the time. The
physical body is the vehicle of the soul and has, as such,
to be fed for the higher purpose of life, to wit, the
advancement of soul. Hunger, says Kabir, is a great
handicap in the path of devotion.*

O Kabir! the dog of hunger spoils meditation by snarls,
Just throw a crumb to it and then sit at ease.

*In the beginning the Satguru teaches a disciple to pray
for his needs, as would appear from the following prayers of Kabir:*

One cannot meditate with hunger gnawing within,
Take thou the rosary away from me, O Lord.[1]

Grant unto me flour, ghee and salt besides some pulse,
That I may have a day's ration to live upon.
A cot, a pillow with a bed and a quilt,
That I may meditate on Thee undisturbed.
I have not been greedy in my demands,
For I love nothing better than Thy Word.[2]

Give unto me as much as I may live on in peace,
And none turns away hungry from my door.

Bhagat Dhanna likewise prayed:

O Lord! I pray unto Thee,
Thou dost supply the needs of thy devotees.
Furnish me with pulse, flour and butter,
That I may happily live in comfort.
Give me clothes and a pair of shoes to wear,
And a good supply of wheat and cereals,
And milch cattle for the supply of milk,
Besides a fine mare to ride on,
And a homely obedient mate in the house;
This is all Dhanna asks for.[3]

*In the Lord's Prayer of Jesus Christ, we have a beautiful
example of all that one need ask:*

Our Father who art in Heaven, Holy is Thy Name,

Thy Kingdom come, Thy Will be done, on Earth as it is
in Heaven.
Give us this day the Bread of Life, and forgive us our
offenses as we forgive those who offend us.
By Thy Spirit lead us out of all temptation, and deliver
us from evil.
For Thine, Thou Everlasting Lord, is the Kingdom, the
Power, and the glory forever.[4]

*Similarly we have a beautiful prayer from the Lord to
the Earthly Mother:*

Our Mother which art upon earth, hallowed be thy
name. Thy Kingdom come, and thy will be done in
us, as it is in thee. As thou sendest every day thy
angels, send them to us also. Forgive us our sins, as
we atone all our sins against thee. And lead us not
into sickness, but deliver us from all evil, for thine is
the earth, the body, and the health.[5]

ESSENE GOSPEL OF JOHN

*The disciples of Buddha, without considering the neces-
sity for formal prayers, have always wished well for all
humanity; and this in fact is the highest type of prayer,
whether we call it prayer or not. Whenever after self-
ablution, they sit in meditation in the morning and evening, they express these thoughts:*

I wish to have universal love for all. I wish that all
creation on all sides—above me and below, on my
right and left—may live in peace. I wish well unto

all, living either in this world or in heaven or in hell. Let there be peace everywhere.

In the Rig Veda (Hindu Scriptures) there are prayers invoking God for the fulfillment of physical and other worldly needs. In Sukat 53 of Mandal 6, we have:

O Lord of valor, we pray for all the gifts of God: for success in our endeavors and the gift of food, and all such things that are desirable. O God of Love, let there be nothing in one's way to gain food in abundance, and have our wishes fulfilled.

In their daily Sandhya, the Hindus recite:

Brahm, the eye of the three regions and the *Devas,* is in front of us. We wish to have him before us for a hundred years, and may we live a hundred years to see him, to hear him, to sing of him, and live for him happily and in prayer, for a hundred years and more.

The Vedantins also think of, dwell upon and meditate on the Mahavakyas (their traditional aphorisms) "Aham Brahm Asmi" (I am Brahm) and "Tat Twam Asi" (I am as Thou art).

The Gayatri—the most sacred Mantra—is a prayer to the Lord to lead us to Him, the Sun of all Light.

Khawaja Hafiz Shirazi, in a state of Divine intoxication, prayed to his Master thus:

Helpless I am and Thou art helpful,
Separated are we for myriads of ages.

In sheer compassion, take me to Thy abode,
Attracted by Thy wondrous beauty, I follow Thee.
Else could I not budge an inch from my place,
Fortunate was Ayaz, the slave of Mahmud,
For having won the kingly favor.
It is a proud privilege to serve at Thy door,
With Thy glance of Grace, make me worthy of it.

Shamas Tabrez prayed to his preceptor as follows:

O Cup-bearer, serve Thou the wine of the other world,
That may give a vision of the Invisible.
A draught whereof may give Divine Intoxication,
And close the critical eyes of the flesh,
And open the mystic eye within.

O Master! ostrich lives on the Kaaf Mountain,
Thou art the true abode of the bird of my soul.
As candle is the altar for the moth,
My life is a thousand times sacrificed on Thee.
Throw down the sluice gates of the waters of life,
And make manifest the fabled spring of *Kausar*.
Grant me the intoxication of love,
And keep my wandering wits at anchor.
My only prayer is that Thou enter and occupy Thy seat
     in the mosque of my body:
And sanctify my poor abode with Thy holy presence.

The set prayer among the Muslims runs:

In the name of God, Most Gracious, Most Merciful.
Praise be to God, the Cherisher and Sustainer of the
     Worlds;

Most Gracious, Most Merciful;
Master of the day of Judgment.
Thee do we worship, and Thine aid we seek.
Show us the straight way, the way of those on whom
    Thou hast bestowed Thy Grace,
Those whose portion is not wrath, and who go not
    astray. Amen!

PRAYERS FROM KABIR

With folded hands I pray: hear, O Ocean of Mercy!
Grant me the gifts of compassion, humility, knowledge
    and happiness, in the company of the saints.
Kabir with thoughts fixed on Thy lotus feet prays,
O Guru! tell me about the True Path of the saints.

What should I ask of Thee? for I feel greatly ashamed,
I commit sins of which Thou art a veritable witness:
    how then can I please Thee?
While I have all the faults in me, Thou art all goodness,
If I may forget Thee, I pray that Thou mayest not
    forget.

O Lord! May I never forget Thee even in the midst of
    millions,
You can have many like me, but for me there is none
    beside Thee,
If I were to forget Thee, where should I get shelter?
I cannot give my heart to others—*Siva, Virancha* or
    Narda.

With all my faults, do not get angry with me, the
    Master doth forgive the lapses of his servant;

Forgetful Kabir is all tainted vile,
But the Master has a loving heart.

I am steeped in sins, sins without number,
It is for Thee to forgive me or to kill me,
Forgive, forgive and again forgive, O Forgiver Divine,
An ever erring child I am, but I depend on the Father's
Grace.
Thou art the abode of infinite virtues with no vice what-
ever,
But when I search my own self, I find myself full of all
ills.
There is not a single virtue in me, listen O Master
Divine!
It is through the Power of Thy Word that I am honored
everywhere.
I am all false, while the Lord is Sterling Truth,
Full of sins as I am, O save me if Thou wilt.

Born with a thistle in my flesh, full of all evils I am,
Thou art the great Donor and Savior, O save me right.
O save me right for I am caught in a great whirlpool,
And shall be carried away by the strong current if Thou
dost not take hold of me.

For other sinners Thou art a well of refreshing waters,
but I am an ocean of sins,
I only depend on the Word of the Master, hear O
Merciful One,
I know not what love is, nor have I any other virtue,
I wonder, how will I have the love of my Beloved?
If I meet the Master, I shall cry out my anguish,

With my head on His feet, I shall speak out my mind.
Permeating all, Thou art immanent in every form,
If I have to leave Thee off, who else will ferry me across?

The ocean of life is too deep to be measured and
sketched,
With thy mercy, O merciful One, I may get a footing.
Full of all evil, I have nothing to boast of and am hard
of heart,
But perfect as my Master is, He can land me ashore.
O my perfect Master! take a firm hold of me,
And lead me to the goal with no break on the way.
Grant me the gift of devotion, O my Munificent One!
I wish for naught, save a ceaseless service unto Thee.
Master! Thou art generous and merciful,
I am drowning in mid-stream, take me over to the shore.

How can the love between Thee and me sever!
As the leaf of the lotus abides in the water, so dost Thou
in Thy servant;
As the night-bird *chakor* gazes at the moon all the
night o'er,
So do I my Lord, thy servant;
From the beginning of time until the ending of time,
there is love between Thee and me,
How can such love be extinguished?
Kabir therefore says: As the river plunges into the ocean,
so doth my heart in Thee.

ODE TO THE SATGURU

Long and dreary has been the struggle of the mind but
all in vain,

All potent art Thou and can do aught, then why this
   delay?
Wandering up and down in the wheel of life, I have
   never had a success,
O Munificent Lord, have mercy, free the spirit and
   concentrate it all,
The arch enemy of the mind is but a waste, O sow in it
   the seeds of love,
Enamored of false delights, it knows not true happiness,
Hankering after the pleasures of the world, it has never
   tasted the sweetness of the Word,
What should I do? How should I try to set it right?
For it does not take to the Word of the Master,
This mind is a curious medley and has no interest in the
   Shabd:
How can it save itself from the vicious cycle of births
   and deaths,
When it does not practice the Word given by the Master?
It shall keep tossing in the world and remain in the
   clutches of *Yama* (the God of Death).
Forgetful of the Word of the Master, it shall suffer
   terribly,
O Master! immanent in every heart, why dost Thou not
   lead me out?
When there is none else whom I can call mine own,
   O take me to the Heaven above,
Have mercy on me now, and take me to Thy Heavenly
   House as Thou may.

Entangled in evil thoughts, I am an utter stranger in a
   strange land,

Reform me this time and I shall lovingly think of Thee
all the time.

I feel repentant and sad as I know not how to contact
my Beloved,

He lives in the High Heavens while I am a creature of
the earth and miserable without Him.

O Satguru! attend to my tale of woe and take me out
of the domain of Death;

In sheer helplessness I cry unto Thee, O hear,

Thou, the Gracious and the Merciful to all but this
unfortunate wretch.

How may I tell Thee of my pain? for I am lying on a
bed of thorns,

Thou, O beloved! hast encouraged me to fly to the
heavens with the wings of love,

Thy Grace has enabled me to meet my Beloved, and
to escape from all toils and miseries.

O Master! just listen to my prayer, I bow unto Thee
again and again:

Drive the evil out of me and grant me proximity to Thy
lotus feet;

Ferry me safely ashore for my barque is in the midst
of an eddying whirl,

None save Thee is my own, save me as Thine own,
O Master!

With all my ills I am yet Thine, and Thou art Donor
beyond all limitations.

I am in great pain, sorrow and affliction, rescue me at
Thy pleasure,

I worship Thee with all my heart and soul, and make
a sacrifice of all unto Thee.
Now I have a powerful sheet anchor though I know not
Thy worth,
Thou hast explained the mystery of the inner Sound
Current but the devil of the mind listens to It not.
Wandering in the ups and downs of life, it runs after
name and fame;
How may I turn its direction without Thy loving Grace,
O Master?
O Lord of my spirit: listen to my prayer, pull the mind
out from its rut.

I ask of the Master but one gift: make me recognize
the mystic Word,
All my life have I wandered with the mind, O free me
from the bondage of Karmas,
Let my Consciousness recede within and hear the ceaseless Sound, and the mind grow still.
Thus can I escape from all ills and reach the eternal
place of Sat Shabd (the true mystic Word).
Grant unto me the intoxication of the Word so that I
may remain absorbed in It.
Then harm and dishonor shall not affect me, for I shall
always be lost in Thy sweet memory.
Let me not be swept off by the time stream, but grant
the sheet anchor of the Word.
My mind has now grown humble, O Master! let it lose
itself in Thy lotus feet.

O Master! take me to Thy abode:

I am a useless fellow, always entangled in doubts and
delusions,

O Thou the Merciful! take me to Thy Abode,

I have no count of the sins I have commited, and my
mind does not catch the Word,

What should I do? My strength fails me and my mind
finds no rest.

O Satguru! take pity on me, for I remain miserable all
the time,

Neither the consciousness recedes within nor the mind
gets stilled, and I cannot appreciate the greatness of
the Word.

I have taken to the Path of the Masters, a High Road
to Spirituality,

Why then O Master dost Thou take no hold of me?

This noble Path of the Masters shall suffer a great set-
back if I succeed not in my endeavors.

I cry from my egoistic reason, and do not resign myself
to Thy Will,

I beg of Thee again and again, O give me the gift of
Thy Word.

O Master, Word personified as Thou art, I come to Thee
for relief.

How can I liberate myself from the wiles of the mind?
This is the problem of my soul.

It has cast a deadly spell of worldly pleasures, and I am
thus separated from my Real Home,

Enmeshed in the ten senses, I find myself in a vicious
circle,

Having been expelled from the tenth portal, I am wandering through the nine gates.

Caught in the web of worldly pleasure, I find no Way out of the bondage,

Besides the Master I see nobody capable enough to lead me out of the wilderness,

I am all afraid of *Yama* (the Lord of Death), who else can free me of this fear?

I have degraded myself to the life of beasts as I have never loved the Master,

As a branch fallen off the tree, I am cast away from the Real Home,

I beg the Master to get my mind to love His lotus feet.

Purify my heart with Thy Satsang; for there it will separate itself from the body and contact the Mystic Sound,

And then will it drink *Amrit* (nectar) from the fount of immortality,

And then will pains and miseries disappear and the soul will have no fear.

Then will I contact the Sound Principle (Word or *Shabd*) and gain the love of my Swami (Lord),

O Lord! make me thine own: I have come, for I seek shelter at Thy feet.[6]

SWAMI SHIV DAYAL SINGH

HYMNS OF MIRA

Herein have I suffered much,
Drive away my sorrow and scepticism.
Now I am in search of Thee, O Lord!
Take me beyond the bounds of affliction,

The whole world is flooding down
The current of births and deaths,
O Lord of Mira—*Gidhar Nagar!*
Rescue her from the giant wheel of births.

I know no peace without seeing Thee, for I know the
deep anguish in my heart,

Over and over again I go to the housetop to see if Thou
art coming; and my eyes have swollen red with
weeping.

The whole world is false and transitory, and so all the
friends and relations;

With folded hands I pray that Thou mayest hear me.

This mind of mine, a great scoundrel, is ever out like
an elephant run amuck.

The Master, having explained the secret, has taken me
in his fold, and I am at rest.

O Girdhar Nagar—the Lord of Mira! I am now fully
absorbed in contemplation of Thee,

Every moment I see Thine immanence everywhere and
seeing I feel blessed.

My friends have turned enemies and hate me, one and
all, but Thou alone art my well-wisher,

My boat is marooned on the high sea, and I feel restless
all the day and get no sleep at night.

By constant waiting and watching have I grown lean
like a thorn,

The arrows of love have pierced my heart and I cannot
for even a moment forget the love pangs.

Thou regained the accursed *Ahilya* from a stone in the
wilderness,

O what complaint is there against Mira—O speak to
me of that.
The perfect Guru, Ravi Das, came from the Supreme
Abode to my rescue,
And He opened up the Way for me, and I became one
with the Lord.

I am being swept down in a fearful current, save me
O Lord, if Thou wilt,
O! none is my own in this world, but Thou alone art
mine.
All friends and relations: one and all,
All are attached to me through selfish ends.
Let the Lord of Mira listen to her supplications.
Grant her the boon of Thy feet, if Thou wilt.

FROM DHANI DHARAM DAS

Grant unto me, O Master, the gift of devotion, for Thou
art a great Donor,
I wish I may not forget Thee all my life and serve Thee
always,
Pilgrimages, fasts and vigils attract me not, nor the
worship of gods;
I have no desire for anything save Thee;
Thou art everything to me, O Possessor of all riches!
I need nothing when I have a Perfect Master by my side;
I would not like even in dream to think of wife, wealth
and children, but of Thee and Thy Greatness.
Listen ye to the prayer of Dharam Das, O the Munifi-
cent Lord!
Take me out of the gyres and make me Thine own.

THE PRAYER OF SURDAS

O Lord! have mercy on me,
Thou Knower of all hearts, I have no virtue in me.
I cannot get rid of my evil, not even momentarily,
I have on my head a heavy load of cunning and deceit.
Entangled amongst wife, son and riches, I have lost my
very self,
O, come to the rescue of Sur, as his barque is about to
sink.

FROM SIKH SCRIPTURES

*There are many beautiful prayers in the Adi Granth
Sahib, the scriptures of the Sikhs. Some examples follow:*

We are severed from Thee through our own deeds:
show mercy and take us unto Thee again,
Having wandered in all directions, tired and worn out
we have come to Thy feet,
Just as a dry cow is of no consequence and vegetables
without moisture go stale and become valueless,
So we, the worthless, have no peace without our Beloved.
If the Beloved reveals Himself not in the house (body),
the house, nay the very town where one lives is like
a desert,
And all the make-up and ornamentation of the body
become useless.
In the absence of the Beloved, all friends and relations
appear like angels of death (*Yamaduts*),
Nanak prayeth: kindly grant me the gift of Thy Holy
Word.
And unite me with the Lord, who abides forever.[7]

My mind yearns for the sight of the Lord, as doth a
thirsty man for water,
My heart is pierced with the love's dart from my Lord
and He alone knows my miserable state.
Whosoever narrates to me the tales of my Beloved, he
alone is a brother unto me,
Come together ye brothers, accept the Master's Word
and sing songs of my Beloved.
O Lord! fulfill Nanak's desire: Grant him Thy holy
vision, the harbinger of peace.

O mother! how can I find my Beloved, the Lord of my
soul?
I am not beautiful, nor wise, nor strong,
I am a stranger come from afar,
I have no riches, nor am I youthful;
Grant this helpless creature Thy shelter (*Sharan*).
I have become love-stricken from endless seeking.
I am wandering about, thirsty for a vision of the Lord,
Now, O Nanak! the most merciful Lord has quenched
my thirst through contact with the saints.[8]

O Ocean of Mercy! always reside in my heart,
Grant me such wisdom that may make me love the Lord,
I ask for the dust of Thy servant's feet, that I may rub it
over and over again on my forehead;
Fallen as I am to the lowest depths, I am sure that I
will be purified by singing Thy praises.
Let Thy Will be sweet unto me, and whatever Thou
doest be pleasant for me;
Whatever Thou givest I should accept with good grace
and not wish for aught else;

Knowing Thee to be always near me, I wish to be the
    dust to Thy servants;
If we get the company of saints, then alone can we attain
    the Lord.
We are always Thy boy-servants, and Thou art our
    Master,
Nanak saith: I am a child and Thou art my father and
    mother,
And Thy Naam in my mouth is just like exhilarating
    nectar.[9]

It is through Thee that I live, forsake me not even for
    a moment,
O grant me but one gift: remove my doubts and protect
    me, my Beloved, Thou the Knower of all secrets;
The wealth of the Word is more than millions of earthly
    kingdoms,
The nectar of Thy Glance is the highest honor for me:
O Omnipotent Beloved! grant me the power to sing
    Thy praises all the time,
O Benefactor of all souls, I take shelter with Thee,
Nanak lovingly sacrifices himself at Thy feet.[10]

Lord, make me the dust of Thy feet, most merciful
    Beloved, the Captivator of my heart,
Be Gracious enough to satisfy this craving of mine.
Thy praises are being chanted in all the ten directions,
Thine all-knowing wisdom is present everywhere;
Those who sing Thy praises, my Creator, shall have no
    regrets when quitting the world.
The contact of the saints relieves us from all bonds and
    pains,

Nanak knows that all pleasures, riches and delights are
of no consequence, without the love of the Lord.[11]

There is none beside Thee, Thou the Creator, and all
happens as Thou desireth,
All my strength is from Thee and so the support of my
mind;
Nanak always meditates on Thee alone.

O Par Brahm, Thou art the highest Benefactor, and
sustaineth all,
Thou art and Thou shalt ever be: Unreachable, Un-
knowable, the Highest and the Endless.
Those who serve Thee are freed from fear and pain.
Through Guru's Grace, Nanak sings Thy praises.

Whatever we see is evolved from Thee, Thou the Ocean
of Goodness, beautiful Lord,
O seeker, remember Him constantly: but the remem-
brance, O Nanak, cometh only through His Grace.
I am a humble servant of one who meditates on Thee,
Company of such a one liberates all the world,
Nanak saith: O Lord! I pray for the luminous dust of
the saints: fulfill this craving of mine.[12]

Thou art a most loving Lord with many disciples like
me,
Thou art an Ocean of Jewels, with depths immeasurable,
Thou, O Supreme Wisdom! be merciful unto me, and
give me understanding to meditate on Thee all the
time,

O my self, do not be vain and proud, but humble like
dust for that is the way to liberation,
The Lord of Nanak is the highest of all, and many like
Nanak serve His Will.[13]

Be gracious, my Lord, that my eyes may behold Thy
Gracious Form,
Give me millions of tongues, my Beloved,
That I may sing Thy *Naam,*
Singing of Thee will save me from the path of *Yama*
and drive away all pain and sorrow:
The Lord permeates the water, earth, ether and every-
thing besides and I see Him everywhere.
All doubts and delusions having vanished, I see the Lord
as the nearest of the near,
O Lord! be merciful to Nanak, that he may have Thy
blessed vision.

My Beloved Lord, grant me millions of ears that I may
hear Thy praises forever,
Hearing it is that purifies the mind and snaps the bond-
age of time,
All bondage ends by constantly meditating on the Ever-
present;
And then comes in rejoicing and True Knowledge,
By constantly repeating His Name (*Naam*) we become
concentrated into an effortless state of Bliss.
Remembrance of the Lord burns away all sins, and evil
thoughts fly as by an enchanter driven,
Nanak prayeth; Lord, be kind, that men may hear the
Voice of the Ever-present Word.

Millions of hands serve Thee, and millions of feet walk
in Thy Path,

Thy Word is the boat to ferry us across the ocean of life
and death,

Whoever sits in that boat crosses the *Bhavsagar* (the
fearful sea of life and death), and is blessed forever,
with no desire unfulfilled,

All the deadly sins vanish giving place to Bliss, and the
Mystic Sound becomes audible,

Whatever the mind desires that comes to pass,

The Unstruck Sound of the Word is a priceless gem,

Nanak saith: Be kind and grant us the boon of treading
Thy Path all the time.

This is the boon, this the honor, this the treasure of
Naam, and fortunate is he who comes by it;

This is the greatest delight and the highest enjoyment,
for one who meditates at His feet:

Now the mind is absorbed in the contemplation of His
feet and has taken shelter in Him, the Creator of all,

Everything is Thine, O Lord! and Thou art mine, O
Merciful One;

I am a worthless fellow and Thou an Ocean of Bliss:
this realization comes through the company of the
saints.

Nanak saith: The Lord hath been kind; my mind is now
absorbed in the sweet contemplation of His lotus feet.

Thou art my Father and Thou art my Mother,

Thou art my relative and Thou art my brother,

Thou art my Protector everywhere,

What fear can I have?
I found Thee out through Thy Merciful Grace:
Thou art my shelter and also my honor,
There is none besides Thee,
Whatever happens is of Thy doing and nothing is of us.[14]

Thou art our Lord and to Thee we pray:
The soul and the body are Thy gifts,
Thou art mother and father to us, and we are Thy
    children:
Through Thy kindness we get immense happiness,
Nobody knows Thy greatness,
Thou art the Highest Lord of all,
Thou art the Sustainer of all creation,
Which is created by Thee and obeys Thy Will.
Thou alone knowest Thy vastness,
Nanak is always pouring himself out in Thy love.[15]

O Benefactor of this unworthy soul! my life, body and
    mind are all Thine,
How can one gauge Thy greatness?
What cleverness can a purchased slave show?
All my body and soul are Thine: O most beautiful and
    attractive Beloved!
I shall give all that I have for a glimpse of Thee,
Thou my Benefactor, O Lord!
I am a poor beggar at thy door, and Thou art ever
    Gracious.
There is nothing that I can do.
O Master! Thou alone art Unreachable and Limitless!
What service can I render?

What words can I utter to please Thee?

How can I have Thy *Darshan* (a look at Thee)?

We cannot know Thy Greatness, nor Thine Existence
Infinite:

My mind is yearning just for a glimpse of Thee.

I persist in begging of Thee without feeling any sense of
shame,

The gift that I may have the luminous dust from the
feet of Thy saints to smear on my face.

The Master showed His mercy, O Nanak!

And the Lord liberated me through His Grace.[16]

Who is ours besides Thee?

O my Beloved, the Sustainer of my life breath.

You only know the inner state of my mind,

And you alone are the Good Friend:

I have derived all happiness from Thee,

O my Master! Unspeakable, Unweighable,

I cannot describe Thy various plays,

O Thou, the Ocean of all Goodness and the source of
real happiness.

Thou art Unreachable, Ever-Present Lord, but becomest
known through the Master's Grace.

Thou hast eliminated all my fears, and have liberated
me after finishing off my egoism,

The fear of life and death is also gone in the company
of the saints;

I touch the feet of the Guru and serve Him.

I sacrifice my whole being a million times for Him
through whose Grace I have crossed the sea of fear;

Nanak saith: I have now found the Beloved.[17]

Thou art my Protector here and hereafter,
Thou nourished me in my mother's womb:
The fire of *Maya* cannot affect those who are intoxi-
     cated with Thy love,
And are absorbed in Thy holy contemplation.
What qualities of Thine can I describe?
I realize Thy presence within my mind and body:
Thou art my Friend and Master,
I know not anyone else besides Thee.
Whomsoever Thou takest under Thy Protection, not a
     breath of the scorching air can touch Him.
Thou art the Lord and in Thy *sharan* (shelter) one gets
     immense happiness.
Thou makest Thyself known through meditation in the
     company of the saints: Thou the Highest, the Limit-
     less and the Priceless.
Thou art my True Master and I Thy humble slave:
Thou art Lord, Thy greatness true,
Nanak sacrifices his all for Thee.[18]

Thou art my boon companion and my Friend,
Thou art my Beloved and my love goes only to Thee,
Thou art my spouse, honor and adornment,
And I cannot live without Thee, even for a while.

Thou art my jewel and my very life,
Thou my Master and my Ruler too,
I shall ever abide by Thy Will
And shall do what Thou willest.
Wherever I look, I see Thee there in fullness.
I will recite with my tongue

Thy Word that made me fearless,
Thou art my great Treasure and *Bhandar* (merchan-
    dise).
Thou art sweetly sweet and the support of my mind,
Thou art my honor and I am absorbed in Thy love.
Thou art my shelter and Thou my support,
I worship Thee in my mind and body after having got
    this secret from the Guru,
The Guru made me firmly established in the One,
O Nanak! the servant of Hari is ever sustained by Hari.[19]

CHERISHING SALVATION

Pray forget not Thy servant; if for nothing else consider
    my previous love of Thee and possess my heart.
Thou art Gracious and Uplifter of the fallen and so look
    not to our faults.
Thou art my soul, my very life breath, and all my riches
    and happiness,
Kindly burn down the veil of egoism that separates me
    from Thee:
How can a fish live without water?
And how an infant without milk?
Nanak is thirsty for the light of Thy lotus feet:
A glimpse of Thee brings in all the happiness that one
    needs.[20]

Blessed is the love which pours itself out on the lotus
    feet of the Beloved;
When most fortunately I found the Perfect One,
I obtained the fruit of millions of austerities and medita-
    tions,

I am a poor slave of Thine and depend upon Thee alone
with nothing else to depend upon.

The repetition of the Lord's Name has banished all my
fears, and with the collyrium of Thy Word (All wisdom), I have been roused from a long drawn sleep of
ignorance,

Thou art fathomless and extremely great, O Lord! the
veritable Ocean of kindness, full of jewels.

Nanak seeks and begs for the Divine *Naam*: he bows at
the feet of the Lord.[21]

Lord be Gracious, and keep me in Thy *sharan* (shelter),
for I know not how to serve Thee, low and ignorant
as I am.

I have the proud privilege to have Thee as my Beloved:

We are all sinners and always commit mistakes, while
Thou art the Benefactor of the worthless.

We run after *Maya* with our back to the Lord for such
are our deeds.

Thou givest us everything in Thy Compassion, while we
are callously ungrateful to Thee,

Entangled in Thy gifts, we forget the Donor Divine.

There is nothing beyond Thee, O my Liberator,

Nanak saith: O I have come to seek Thy shelter, liberate
this muddle-headed one also.[22]

O Hari! save me from disgrace, as I am greatly afraid
of *Yama* (Death).

I have come to Thy *sharan*, O Ocean of mercy:

I am foolish and greedy and I have run myself out in
sinning and sinning;

The fear of death haunts me in and out all the time.

I am being consumed in the invisible fires within.
I have tried many remedies to obtain salvation,
And have searched in all the ten directions,
But the secrets of the Lord residing within, I could not
find.
Devoid of all virtues, I have done no meditation nor
undergone any austerities,
What should I do now?
O Nanak! exhausted and defeated as thou art,
Seek thou His anchorage and pray for the boon of fear-
lessness.[23]

Do hear my prayer, O my Lord!
I am Thy disciple even if filled with millions of sins,
Thou art the Destroyer of all ills: ever kind and bewitch-
ing, the Dispeller of sorrows and woes,
Grant me shelter at Thy feet, and protect me, O Thou
the All-Pervading Absolute.
Seated in the hearts of all, Thou art both seeing and
hearing us through, for Thou art nearer than the
nearest,
O Lord! do hear Nanak's prayer: save me, for I am
Thy disciple.
Thou art ever All-Powerful, while we are poor beggars
entangled in worldly attractions.
O, do take us out of the mire and free us from the
bondage of mind and matter,
For we are every moment paying the penalty for our
faults:
O my Creator, Thou art unattached and free from all
limitations.

Tired as I am from wanderings into many incarnations,
O have mercy upon me,
Nanak prayeth: I am the slave of Hari:
The Lord is the support of my life breath.

Thou art All-Powerful, while I have inferior intelligence,
　　my Lord;
Thou, however, providest even for the ungrateful,
Perfect as Thou art in Thy Merciful Vision:
O Creator, Thou art Beyond all understanding and
　　Limitless, while I am lowly and know naught:
With my back upon the pearls, I collect shells,
Brute, low and ignorant as I am,
The hard earned *maya* (wealth), collected through
　　means fair and foul, is transitory and disappears in
　　the twinkling of an eye.
Nanak seeks the shelter of the Omnipotent One,
Do save me from ultimate disgrace.[24]

We are dirty, Thou Pure: we are so unworthy of Thee,
　　O Benefactor,
We are fools, while thou art All Wisdom and Possessor
　　of all powers (arts).
O Madho, what a world of difference between the two;
We the failing ones and Thou so perfect:
We the sinners, and Thou the Destroyer of all sins,
　　O beautiful Beloved:
Thou hast created everything and hast provided for
　　everyone with life, body and soul,
This worthless one is without qualities, and yet Thou
　　givest him all out of Thy kindness.

Thou doest good which we do not appreciate and yet
   Thou art always kind,
O Lord! protect Thy children, Thou the treasure of
   everything and an ever-abiding King.
The creation begs of Thee:
Nanak saith: Low as we are, save us for the sake of
   Thy saints.[25]

Make me Thine own, O Merciful One, for I have taken
   shelter at Thy door,
Save me, O Benefactor of the poor, I have tired myself
   out in quest of Thee,
It is in Thy very nature to love Thy devotees and to
   lift up the fallen:
There is no one else save Thee to hearken to my prayer,
I pray, take me up, O Merciful One, and get me out
   of the ocean of *Sansara* by holding my hand.[26]

O my Beloved; hear how I wander alone in the wilder-
   ness!
How can I have patience without the Beloved? the
   Carefree as He is.
A wife cannot live without her spouse during the long
   and tortuous nights;
I do not get a wink of sleep, I only yearn for my love,
   O listen to me.
In the absence of the Beloved, none has any sympathy
   for me, and I cry all alone.
Nanak saith: the wife doth get her Beloved if she really
   feels unhappy and is extremely miserable without him.

The Beloved of my life has left me, who is there to
   unite me with Him?

There is happiness when love unites, for then the Word
(Mystic Sound) becomes pleasant.

When the Word doth become blissful, we get the right
place, with the inner (mystic) lamp illumining the
body.

Hear, my friend, we become really beautiful by singing
the praises of the Supreme Truth.

When Satguru united me with the Beloved, I got the
pleasure of His company

And the Divine Word full of nectar made me buoyant
with happiness.

Nanak says: a wife can have true happiness, when the
Beloved is also fond of her;

Though forgetful of Thee, we are still Thine own, O
Lord!

Even if I commit mistakes, still I have the proud privilege to belong to Thee,

He whose mind has gone elsewhere, will surely die from
the very regret of having done so.

How can I leave the side of my Beloved, when I see
that He is the Sustainer of my soul?

Thou art my friend and relation, and I am highly proud
of Thee,

When Thou art in, I am happy and feel that my poor
self is honored.

Now that Thou hast been so kind to me,

Pray let me not look anywhere else, and

Let me keep the gift of Thy remembrance ever locked
in my heart.

I will walk down leagues to have Thy *Darshan* (a love
glance),
I will love to hear Thy stories should it please Thee and
the Satguru,
Millions of suns and moons cannot equal the glory of
Thy one hair;
Thou art the greatest of the Great: the Indescribable
and the Ineffable.
I cannot praise Thee sufficiently: Thy friends run into
millions and all superior to me,
Just bestow one Gracious Look on me, and I will be
the happiest creature.

By seeing Him, the mind gets Supreme Peace, and all
mental ills leave off,
How can I forget Him Who saturates me with His
Divine Presence?
With great humility I threw myself at His feet, and
He made me His own for the asking.
Nanak got Him through the help of a Saint, for it was
so preordained.[28]

Thou art my Father, Thou art my Mother,
Thou art my soul and life, O Bestower of Happiness:
Thou art my Master, and I am Thy slave,
And apart from Thee nothing is mine.
Grant that I may be singing Thy praises day and night:
We are Thine instruments and Thou playest on them.
We are beggars at Thy door, give us the Gift,
O our Benefactor!
Through Thy Grace I may enjoy inner Bliss,

For Thou art permeating every heart.
Through Thy Grace alone one can repeat Thy sweet
    Naam,
And sing Thy praises in the company of Thy beloved
    saints.
Through Thy Mercy, our pains are eliminated,
And through Thy Grace, the lotus of the heart opens
    out.
I lovingly pour myself out at the feet of the *Gurdev* (the
    Radiant Form of the Master),
Whose *Darshan* (sight) is fruitful and whose service so
    purifying.
Be kind, O my Lord! that Nanak may sing Thy praises
    constantly.[29]

My Lord, what a poor helpless fellow am I!
Thou hast raised me into a man from a very low birth,
And therein lies Thy greatness.
Thou art the Lord of all, the Giver of soul and the life-
    breath,
And none can describe Thy numerous attributes.
Beloved of all, Thou providest nourishment to all, Thou
    the Sustainer of all life,
None knows Thy mystery permeating as Thou art unto
    the vastness and the Beyond, for all this is Thy mani-
    festation,
Nanak prayeth: Grant me the ship of the saints' com-
    pany to cross the ocean of life and death.[30]

Keep us as it pleaseth Thee, we have come unto Thy
    shelter.

We commit mistakes day and night, and the Lord
   forgives us and protects our honor,
We are Thy ever-erring children, and Thou art our
   Guru and Father,
O give us good advice:
Nanak is Thy servant, save Him from disgrace.[31]

IMPLORING THE UNEQUALED BOON OF NAAM

Satguru, I have come to Thy feet:
Give me the bliss of *Naam* for Divine honor and free
   me from all anxieties.
I cannot think of any other place of rest, and as a last
   resort, I am at Thy door,
Whether I deserve it or not, O save me as Thou wilt,
   for merit I have none.
Thou art ever forgiving, ever kind and sustaineth all,
Nanak hath taken his refuge with the saints: kindly
   protect him this time.[32]

I get real life from a vision of Thy Divine Face, and feel
   myself fortunate indeed,
Hear this prayer of mine, my Lord:
Make me Thy disciple and give me the gift of *Naam*,
And keep me under Thy protection, my Benevolent
   Lord:
It is only the rare few who appreciate the Guru's Grace,
Hear my appeal, my Lord and Friend:
Let Thy lotus feet abide in my heart,
Nanak makes but one request:
Do not slip away from my remembrance,
O Thou, the Ocean of All-Goodness.[33]

O Lord! be kind and grant that we may sing Thy
praises,
I wistfully wait for the time when the Lord will hug
me to His bosom.
We are children without wisdom and are steeped in stark
ignorance,
Thou our Father, make us understand.
Sons commit mistakes again and again, while the Father
of us all still loves them.
Whatever, O Lord! whatever Thou givest us, we gladly
accept it, for we have no other shelter whereto we
may turn.
The Lord shall be dear to such devotees, who are dear
to the Lord,
Through Thy Grace, we shall merge ourselves into Thee,
Through Thy Grace alone can we constantly remember
Thee,
Nanak has come to Hari's door,
He will save me from disgrace.[34]

FOR GRANTING SOLEMN CHANCE TO SERVE SAINTS AND FOR SELF-SURRENDER TO THE LORD

O Merciful One, I ask of Thee to make me a slave of
Thy servants:
When Thou speakest to me, I feel alive, and get all
wealth and kingdoms.
The treasure of *Naam* nectar is plentiful in the house of
the Lord's devotees,
I feel elated in their company for there I hear His
praises,

My body gets purified in their service.
I bring water for them, fan them, grind their corn and
get happy by washing their feet,
I cannot do anything of myself.
Show me Thy Grace, O Lord!
Give me a place to live with the Divine Saints.[35]

O show me Thy Gracious Face, that I may sing Thy
praises at dusk and dawn and dust the feet of Thy
servants with the long hair of my head,
That is my inner desire, O Master! for there is none
besides Thee that I may think of.
I meditate on Thy lotus feet, and look toward Thee:
Merciful Lord! the Master of all.
With folded hands I pray, that Nanak,
Thy servant, may repeat Thy Divine *Naam,*
And get into the Beyond in the twinkling of an eye.[36]

O Lord! I have just one desire:
O Treasure of mercy and benevolence, make me a
disciple of Thy saints;
I may make obeisance unto them at early morning
hours,
And reverently look at their beaming faces day and
night,
And dedicate myself, body and mind to their service;
I may ever sing praises of the Lord with my tongue, and
With each breath of my life, let me remember the Lord,
and let me live with the saints from day to day.
My only food and wealth is Thy Divine *Naam,*
Thus Nanak enjoys real bliss.[37]

Do me one favor: let my forehead be at the feet of the
   saints,
My eyes have His Darshan (look),
My body lie in the luminous dust of His Feet,
The Word of the Guru surge in my heart,
And the Name of the Lord abide in me.
Liberate me from the five deadly sins (lust, anger, greed,
   attachment and egoism),
And burn all my doubts and delusions, O Master,
Whatever you do we may take it to be for our good
   without any regrets whatsoever.
You are the Benefactor of Nanak, O Lord!
Liberate me through the company of Thy saints.[38]

For Shelter From Five Passions

My Father save me: I am without any virtue,
While Thou art All Virtuous; I am all alone and have
   to contend with five enemies.
Protect me, O my Savior! the foes play hell with me
   and make me terribly miserable,
I have come therefore to Thy *sharan* (shelter).
I have tried all *sadhnas* to avoid them, but they do not
   leave me.
Having heard of the protective power of the Saints, I
   have come to them for relief,
They were kind enough to come to my rescue and I
   found great relief through them.
The Saints gave me a lesson in fearlessness and I prac-
   ticed their Word:
Thus I did conquer the fearful foes through the blissful
   Bani (the Mystic Sound),

Nanak says: Having seen the Light I have attained the
Deep Stillness.[39]

Thou makest me free from passions, falsehood, greed
and speaking ill of others;
Weed all the evil propensities out of me and call me
near to Thee;
And make me the knower of Thy Will.
Hari's servants sing songs of happiness;
O teach me the way whereby I may never forget Thee
even for a moment.
Most fortunately, Nanak met the Perfect Guru,
And since then his mind has ceased to wander any-
where.[40]

I know none other than Thee:
Thou art with me, Thou my friend and companion,
O Lord!
What fear can I have with Thee as my sheet anchor
and my hope?
Let me not forget Thee for a moment, even while I sit
or stand and am in bed or out of it:
Keep me always in Thy *sharan* (protection), for
This world is a dreadful ocean of fire,
O Nanak's Satguru! Thou art the giver of real hap-
piness;
And we are Thy children, O Lord![41]

GENERAL: PRAYERS FOR ALL

All the sins of the saint's devotees who serve the Lord
are eliminated and done away with,

Be kind to us, O Lord! and keep us in the company of
those dear to Thee.

My Lord! I cannot describe Thy Greatness,

With the dead weight of sins like millstones around us,
we were sinking in midstream, when Thou so graciously lifted us out.

For many incarnations we were entangled in the obnox-
ious lures of the world, but when we came into contact
with the saints, we were saved.

As gold is purified by heating in the fire, so does our
dirty mind get etherealized.

Recite His *Naam* day and night, and make your heart
saturated with the love of Hari,

His *Naam* is a perfect remedy in this world:

Our egoism too was finished up by the Power of His
holy Word;

Hari is unique and beyond our understanding and still
beyond the beyond,

O the Infinitely Conscious Personality,

Be Thou kind to Thy servant;

Nanak has come to Thy shelter.[42]

We are blind and blindly entangled in the stupefying
enjoyments of the senses,

How can we follow the Path of the Guru?

Only through the Grace of the True Teacher can we
join His fold.[43]

There is none so poor as I am and none more merciful
than Thou art,

What then is needed?

I have but an unsteady mind:

O lead me to a Perfect Saint.
When I pour out all my love for the Lord,
Why art Thou so silent, O Madho?
We have been separated from *Sach Khand* for many an
incarnation;
But this life I dedicate to Thee.
Ravidas says: I live in the hope of having Thy sacred
Darshan (a meeting),
Which I have not had for such a long time.[44]

What qualities of Thine can we describe?
O Master! Thou art Limitless and beyond all descrip-
tion.
We sing praises of Thy Naam day and night and that is
our only hope.
We are ignorant and do not know how to cross over to
Thee.
The lowly Nanak is His bondsman and a drawer of
water,
Make us live as Thou pleaseth, for now we live under
Thy shelter,
We commit mistakes at every step,
But Thou art the Forgiver and Keeper of our honor,
We are Thy ignorant children, and Thou art our Father
and Master:
O Teach us the Way:
He took Nanak out of serfdom
And has accepted him as His own.[45]

O Master, have mercy upon us,
And take us to Thyself.

We are but worthless cargo,
And Thou canst pilot us to our End.[46]

O Master, come and unite me,
Who has been long separated from my Lord;
My body and mind have been emptied of attachment,
O fill me with the Light of God.[47]

Having renounced all things,
I have come to Thee, my Master;
O take me under Thy wings,
And make of me what Thou wilt.[48]

The Master is the true devotee of the Lord,
And so to Him I pray;
We are but worthless creatures and seek Thy protection,
O grant us the gift of Thy Word.[49]

Seeing the world in flames,
We turned to the Lord for refuge;
O Master, save us and deliver us,
For therein lies God's Glory.[50]

I am purifying my heart,
To make it fit for Thy Altar,
O True Friend! I have come to seek Thy refuge,
Teach me the Way to God.[51]

Thou alone knowest Thy mysteries,
For Thou art all complete;
O give refuge to a worthless orphan,
And lead him to his destined goal.[52]

I pray to my Master to unite me to my Lord,
Meeting whom I may find peace and freedom from
    death.[53]

When I prayed for the company of the saints,
Hearing me the Lord's true devotee came unto me;
It was my good fortune that they made me their own.[54]

Nanak prays to the Master that he may be united with
    God.[55]

O my Beloved, grant me the holy Word of God.
Those that have full faith in the Master, their worries
    are over.[56]

O Master, we have come to Thy fold,
To have the peace of the Divine Word,
And the Grace of God,
And a riddance from all our cares.[57]

May I live beholding Thee, O my Master,
And may my deeds bear fruit;
This is our prayer to Thee, O Lord,
Grant us the boon of Thy Word and make us Thine
    own.[58]

This is my only prayer to Thee,
That I, lost in Thy meditation, be dyed in Thy color.[59]

Thou Giver of all gifts, grant me this boon,
That I may be freed from vanity and ego, from lust,
    greed and wrath.[60]

FROM BOOK OF COMMON PRAYER

The following prayers have been selected from the Book of Common Prayer as used by the clergy and laity of the Church of England. These will serve as inspired examples of spiritual devotion, reverence, humility, supplication and praise to the Supreme Creator. Such sublime incentives are inherent in all religions, establishing the universality of a common origin and destiny for all mankind.

O God, the strength of them all that put their trust in Thee, mercifully accept our prayers; and because through the weakness of our mortal nature we can do no good thing without Thee, grant us the help of thy Grace, that in keeping of Thy commandments we may please Thee, both in will and deed; through Jesus Christ our Lord. Amen.

O Lord, Who never failest to help and govern them whom Thou dost bring up in Thy steadfast fear and love; Keep us, we beseech Thee, under the protection of Thy good providence, and make us to have a perpetual fear and love of Thy holy name, through Jesus Christ our Lord. Amen.

O Lord, we beseech Thee mercifully to hear us; and grant that we, to whom Thou has given a hearty desire to pray, may by Thy mighty aid be defended and comforted in all dangers and adversities; through Jesus Christ our Lord. Amen.

O God, the Protector of all who trust in Thee, without Whom nothing is strong, nothing is holy; increase and multiply upon us Thy mercy; that Thou being our ruler and guide, we may so pass through things temporal, that we finally lose not the things eternal. Grant this, O heavenly Father, for Jesus Christ's sake our Lord. Amen.

Grant, O Lord, we beseech Thee, that the course of this world may be so peaceably ordered by Thy governance, that Thy Church may joyfully serve Thee in all godly quietness; through Jesus Christ our Lord. Amen.

O God Who hast prepared for them that love Thee such things as pass man's understanding; Pour into our hearts such love towards Thee, that we, loving Thee above all things, may obtain Thy promises, which exceed all that we can desire, through Jesus Christ our Lord. Amen.

Lord of all power and might, Who art the Author and Giver of all good things; Graft in our hearts the love of Thy Name, increase in us true religion, nourish us with all goodness, and of Thy great mercy keep us in the same; through Jesus Christ our Lord. Amen.

O God, who declarest Thine Almighty Power most chiefly in showing mercy and pity; Mercifully grant unto us such a measure of Thy Grace, that we, running the way of Thy commandments, may obtain Thy gracious promises, and be made partakers of Thy heavenly treasure; through Jesus Christ our Lord. Amen.

Almighty and Everlasting God, Who art always more ready to hear than we to pray, and are wont to give more than either we desire or deserve; Pour down upon us the abundance of Thy mercy; forgiving us those things whereof our conscience is afraid, and giving us those good things which we are not worthy to ask, but through the merits and meditation of Jesus Christ, Thy Son, our Lord. Amen.

Almighty and Merciful God, of whose only gift it cometh that Thy faithful people do unto Thee true and laudable service; Grant, we beseech Thee, that we may so faithfully serve Thee in this life, that we fail not finally to attain Thy heavenly promises; through the merits of Jesus Christ our Lord. Amen.

Almighty and Everlasting God, give unto us the increase of faith, hope and charity and that we may obtain that which Thou dost promise, make us to love that which Thou dost command; through Jesus Christ our Lord. Amen.

Keep, we beseech Thee, O Lord, Thy Church with Thy perpetual mercy; and because of the frailty of man without Thee cannot but fail, keep us ever by Thy help, from all things hurtful, and lead us to all things profitable to our salvation; through Jesus Christ our Lord. Amen.

O Lord, we beseech Thee, let Thy continual pity cleanse and defend Thy Church; and because it cannot

continue in safety without Thy succor, preserve it ever-
more by Thy help and goodness; through Jesus Christ
our Lord. Amen.

Lord, we beseech thee, grant Thy people Grace to
withstand the temptations of the world, the flesh and
the Devil, and with our pure hearts and minds to follow
Thee the only God; through Jesus Christ our Lord.
Amen.

O God, for as much as without Thee we are not able
to please Thee; mercifully grant, that Thy Holy Spirit
may in all things direct and rule our hearts; through
Jesus Christ our Lord. Amen.

O Almighty and Most Merciful God, of Thy bountiful goodness keep us; that we, being ready both in body
and soul, may cheerfully accomplish those things that
Thou wouldst have done; through Jesus Christ our
Lord. Amen.

Grant, we beseech Thee, Merciful Lord, to Thy faithful people pardon and peace, that they may be cleaned
from all sins, and serve Thee with a quiet mind; through
Jesus Christ our Lord. Amen.

Lord, we beseech Thee to keep Thy household the
Church in continual godliness, that through Thy protection it may be free from all adversities, and devoutly
given to serve Thee in good works, to the glory of Thy
Name; through Jesus Christ our Lord. Amen.

O God, our refuge and strength, Who art the author of all goodness; be ready, we beseech thee, to hear the devout prayers of Thy Church; and grant that those things which we ask faithfully we may obtain effectually; through Jesus Christ our Lord. Amen.

O Lord, we beseech Thee, absolve thy people from their offenses; that through Thy bountiful goodness we may all be delivered from the hands of those sins which by our frailty we have committed: grant this, O Heavenly Father, for Jesus Christ's sake, our blessed Lord and Savior. Amen.

Prayer for Selflessness

Lord, make me an instrument of thy peace; where there is hatred, let me sow love; where there is injury, pardon; where there is doubt, faith; where there is despair, hope; where there is darkness, light; and where there is sadness, joy.

O Divine Master, grant that I may not so much seek to be consoled as to console; to be understood as to understand; to be loved as to love; for it is in giving that we receive; it is in pardoning that we are pardoned; and it is in dying that we are born to eternal life.

ST. FRANCIS OF ASSISI

Bedtime Prayer

O Heavenly Father, protect and bless all things that have breath; guard them from all evil and let them sleep in peace.

ALBERT SCHWEITZER

SPRINGTIME PRAYER

Now winter is gone, and spring is here: now tiny leaves, and blossoms sweet, lambs in the fields, and baby calves, and budding flowers about my feet. O teach me gentleness, please God, to care for all things weak and small, that I may grow strong and brave and helpful in my love for all.

ANONYMOUS

We may conclude this section with the following few prayers:

Almighty God, unto Whom all hearts be open, all desires known, and from Whom no secrets are hid; cleanse the thoughts of our hearts by the inspiration of Thy Holy Spirit, that we may perfectly love Thee, and worthily magnify Thy Holy Name; through Jesus Christ our Lord. Amen.

O Lord Christ, we, Thy faithful soldiers, dedicate this newborn day to Thee, praying that it may shine in Thy service as a pure pearl in the chaplet of our life, O Thou Great King of Love, to whom be praise and adoration forevermore. Amen.

Teach us, O Lord, to see Thy life in all men and in all the peoples of Thine earth, and so guide the nations into the understanding of Thy laws that peace and good will may reign upon earth; through Christ our Lord. Amen.

To the most Holy and adorable Trinity, Father, Son and Holy Spirit, Three Persons in One God; to Christ our Lord, The Only Wise Counselor, the Prince of Peace; to the Seven Mighty Spirits before the Throne; and to the glorious Assembly of just men made perfect, the Watchers, the Saints, the Holy Ones, be praise unceasing from every living creature; and honor, might and glory, henceforth and forevermore. Amen.

The Peace of God, which passeth all understanding, keep your hearts and minds in the knowledge and love of God, and of His Son, Christ our Lord; and the blessing of God Almighty, the Father, the Son, and the Holy Ghost, be amongst you, and remain with you always. Amen.

> Midst Thy circling power I stand,
> On every side I find Thy hand,
> Awake, asleep, at home, abroad,
> I am surrounded still with God.
>
> Let these thoughts possess my breast
> Wherever I roam, wherever I rest,
> Let not my weaker passions dare
> Consent to sin, for God is there.

PRAYERS FROM VARIOUS RELIGIONS

From Hindu Scriptures

Om: The Thousand-headed *Purusha*, thousand-eyed, thousand-footed, even He, encompassing the Universe on all sides, remained over ten fingers in extent. *Purusha* alone is all this, that which has been and that which is to be. Moreover, He is the Director of immortality; and hence manifests Himself as the Universe evolving by means of food. Of this magnitude is His greatness, even greater than this is *Purusha*. One fourth of Him forms all created things, the Immortal three fourths are in the regions above.

One God sits hidden in every creature, pervading all, the Inmost Self of all beings, the Watcher over all acts, abiding in all created things, the Witness, the Heart, the Absolute, Free of all attributes.

The One Dweller, Self-controlled, who divided the One Seed into the Many, who is their *Atma*, those steadfast ones see Him enthroned with their Atma; for them alone is Bliss Eternal, not for others.

That blessing do we choose, in order that we may sing for the purposes of the sacrifice, and for the Lord of the sacrifice. Divine blessing be ours. May blessing be on the children of men. May that which is of good effect go always singing upward. May blessing be on us, the two-footed, blessing on the four-footed. Om! Peace, Peace, Peace!

From Zoroastrian Scriptures

1. We pray for the gracious joy of God the Omniscient Lord of Existence. Beneficent Holiness is the best of blessings. It alone is the source of true happiness. Happiness to him who is sincerely righteous.

2. O Lord! Through the most beneficent and excellent Path of Purity may we see Thee, face to face. May we then observe Thy many aspects. And may we be finally merged into Thy Benign Presence.

3. Cleanse Thou my soul, O Omniscient and most Bountiful Spirit! Grant me strength through Perfect Wisdom, goodness through devotion, courage through righteousness, and leadership through Benevolent Mind. In order that I may acquire spiritual knowledge to instruct others, grant me that power, which is indeed the resulting blessing from the Lord of Benevolence. Reveal unto me the laws of religion through upright mind and pure conduct. Then does Zoroaster give away, in charity, even his own life besides his perfect benevolent Wisdom, to the Omniscient Lord. He dedicates his power of speech and action, to serve *Asha* (Holy Divine Spirit) and *Sraosha* (the angel of inspiration).

4. As is *Ahu* (the High Ruler) absolute in His Will, so is the Spiritual Teacher *Ratu* wielding authority through the law of righteousness. The reward of good deeds, done as offering unto the Lord, is the gift of Benevolent Mind. Whoever gives protecting help to the needy, is entitled to receive power from the Creator.

5. O Omniscient God: when malicious people seek to harm me, who else shall grant me protection, except the Divine Fire and Wisdom that are within me? Indicate to me, O God! the good deeds that may propagate righteousness in this world. In order that I may expound to others the teachings of the good Faith, tell me, O

Lord! how the evil forces may be foiled. Surely Thy protecting words that are eternal will prevail. Reveal unto me a teacher, who may be full of Wisdom, and proficient in the lore of both the worlds, so innocent that the Angel of Inspiration may aproach him through his loving thoughts. A true teacher is Thy beloved agent.

6. O Immortal: Archangel: I offer unto you my sacrifice and devotion through thought, word and deed, and with all my heart I dedicate the very life of my existence. I adore the Path of Purity.

7. Whoever amongst the living beings is foremost in loving sacrifice, is always within the knowledge of the Lord, because of his righteous conduct. We pay our homage unto all such men and women who have sought to serve.

FROM JAIN SCRIPTURES

Reverence to the Arhats,
Reverence to the Perfect Ones,
Reverence to the Heads of the Sangha,
Reverence to the Preceptors,
Reverence to all holy Monks in the World.

All these five are worthy of Reverence. They are all protectors against sin. Among all auspicious things, this is the most auspicious.

FROM HEBREW SCRIPTURES

Hear O Israel, the Lord is our God, the Lord is One. May it be Thy will, O Lord our God, and of our fathers, to cause us to walk in Thy Law and cleave to Thy commandments; and lead us not into sin, transgression, temptation and contempt. Remove from us every evil inclination and cause us to adhere to the good.

O, grant us grace, favor and mercy in Thy sight, and in the sight of all that behold us; and bestow gracious favors on us. Blessed art Thou, O Lord, who bestowest gracious favors on Thy people Israel. Amen.

(The word "Israel" is composed of ISR (Righteous), EL (Omnipotent); hence means: those who righteously walk in the Law of God.)

FROM BUDDHIST SCRIPTURES

Praise be to the Lord, the Holy One, Perfect in Wisdom.
Praise be to the Lord, the Holy One, Perfect in Wisdom.
Praise be to the Lord, the Holy One, Perfect in Wisdom.

I go to the Buddha for refuge,
I go to the Law for refuge,
I go to the Brotherhood for refuge.

For the second time, I go to the Buddha for refuge,
For the second time, I go to the Law for refuge,
For the second time, I go to the Brotherhood for refuge.

For the third time, I go to the Buddha for refuge,
For the third time, I go to the Law for refuge,
For the third time, I go to the Brotherhood for refuge.

I promise to abstain from taking the life of any living creature.

I promise to abstain from taking anything with thievish intent.

I promise to abstain from the evil indulgence of bodily passions.

I promise to abstain from falsehood.

I promise to abstain from any intoxicating liquor or drug.

FROM THEOSOPHY

Invocation by all

O Hidden Life! vibrant in every atom;
O Hidden Light! shining in every creature;
O Hidden Love! embracing all in Oneness;
May each who feels himself as one with Thee,
Know he is also one with every other.

ANNIE BESANT

REFERENCES

References

1. Maru War M.5
2. Sri Rag M.1
3. Gauri M.5
4. Todi M.5
5. Sri Rag M.5
6. Gauri M.5
7. War Sri Rag M.4
8. Asa M.5
9. Suhi M.4
10. Gujri M.5
11. Al-Umar:Ayat 9-10
12. Maru M.5
13. Amos 3:7
14. Gauri M.5
15. *Ibid.*
16. *Ibid.*
17. Gujri M.5
18. John 15:16
19. John 14:14
20. Matthew 7:11
21. Bilawal M.5
22. Asa M.5
23. Dhanasri M.5
24. Malar M.5
25. Matthew 7:7-8
26. Dev M.5
27. John 14:15
28. John 15:7
29. Psalm 37:4
30. Matthew 6:12, 14-15
31. Psalm 103:13
32. Mark 9:24
33. Suhi M.5
34. Matthew 6:8
35. Asa M.5
36. Asa M.4
37. Kalyan M.4
38. Maru War M.2
39. Bhairon M.5
40. Akal Ustat
41. Asa M.2
42. Acts 17:24
43. Al-Bakr
44. I Corinthians 3:16
45. Parbhati M.3
46. Matthew 6:6
47. Maru War M. 5
48. Gauri M.5
49. *Ibid.*
50. Matthew 6:22
51. John 14:9, 11
52. Ramkali M.1
53. Jap Ji
54. Jap Ji
55. Maru M.1
56. Jaitsari Ravidas
57. Jap Ji
58. Gauri M.5
59. Dhanasri M.5
60. Dhanasri Kabir
61. Gauri M.5
62. Bihagra War M.5
63. Gond Namdev
64. Matthew 5:8
65. Matthew 6:22
66. Gauri M.5
67. Suhi M.4
68. Gauri M.5
69. *Ibid.*
70. Shalok M.5
71. Gauri Kabir
72. Gauri M.5
73. Majh M.5
74. Dhanasri Ravidas

151

75. Dhanasri M.3
76. Gauri M.5
77. Jaitsari M.5
78. Suhi War M.3
79. War Ramkali M.5
80. Vadhans M.3
81. Asa Kabir
82. Asa M.5
83. Sarang M.5
84. Bilawal M.5
85. Suhi M.1
86. Tilang M.1
87. Sorath M.5
88. Suhi M.5
89. Jaitsari M.5
90. Asa M.5
91. Bhairon M.1
92. Dhanasri Ravidas
93. Suhi M.4
94. *Ibid.*
95. Bilawal M.4
96. Asa M.4
97. Ramkali M.5
98. Gauri M.5
99. *Ibid.*
100. Tokhari M.1
101. Gauri M.5
102. *Ibid.*
103. Shalok M.3
104. Gauri M.1
105. Bilawal War M.3
106. Suhi M.5
107. Kalyan M.4
108. Bilawal M.4
109. Bilawal M.3
110. Ramkali M.5
111. Kanra M.5
112. Dhanasri M.5
113. Gujri M.4
114. Basant M.9
115. Sar Bachan 216
116. Bilawal M.1
117. Jap Ji 16
118. Asa M.5
119. *Ibid.*

120. Sorath M.5
121. Kanra M.4
122. Asa M.5
123. Shalok Kabir
124. Malar M.5
125. Bilawal M.5
126. Asa M.5
127. Gauri M.4
128. Kanra M.4
129. Bhairon M.4
130. Suhi M.4
131. Gujri M.5
132. Maru M.4
133. Prabhati M.3
134. Suhi M.5
135. Dhanasri M.3
136. Dhanasri M.5
137. Gujri M.5
138. Bihagra M.5
139. Kalyan M.4
140. Gauri M.3
141. Amos 3:7
142. II Timothy 3:16
143. John 1:12
144. John 14:10
145. John 5:25
146. John 5:43
147. John 6:44
148. Bihagra-ki-War M.4
149. John 8:12
150. John 1:1-5
151. Maru M.5
152. Malar M.5
153. Todi M.5
154. Maru M.4
155. Suhi M.5
156. Telang M.1
157. Gujri M.4
158. War 36, Pauri 28
159. Suhi M.4
160. Gauri M.5
161. Sri Rag M.1
162. Suhi M.5
163. Bilawal M.5
164. Vadhans M.3

Appendix

1. Shalok Kabir
2. Sorath Kabir
3. Dhanasri Dhanna
4. Manual of Prayer (May 1957), page 15
5. Essene Gospel of John (E. B. Szekely, trans.) 22:1-39
6. Sar Bachan
7. Bara Maha 133
8. Gauri M.5
9. Todi M.5
10. *Ibid.*
11. *Ibid.*
12. Tilang M.5
13. Suhi M.5
14. Majh M.5
15. Gauri M.5
16. Suhi M.5
18. Majh M.5
19. Gauri M.5
20. Bilawal M.5
21. Kanra M.5
22. Bilawal M.5
23. Jaitsari M.9
24. Bihagra M.5
25. Sorath M.5
26. War Jaitsari M.5
27. Gauri M.1
28. Suhi M.5
29. Bhairon M.5
30. Sarang M.5
31. Asa M.4
32. Todi M.5
33. Suhi M.5
34. Kalyan M.4
35. Gujri War M.5
36. *Ibid.*
37. Dev Gandhari M.5
38. Bilawal M.5
39. Gauri M.5
40. Sorath M.5
41. Asa M.5
42. Dhanasri M.4
43. Dhanasri M.5
44. Dhanasri Ravidas
45. Asa M.4
46. Malar M.4
47. Asa M.4
48. Suhi M.5
49. Gujri M.5
50. Vadhans M.3
51. Sorath M.5
52. Gauri M.5
53. Sri Rag M.1
54. Todi M.5
55. Suhi M.1
56. Sarang M.4
57. Todi M.5
58. Suhi M.5
59. Bilawal M.5
60. Suhi M.1

OTHER BOOKS

BY KIRPAL SINGH

Godman: Finding a Spiritual Master
The Crown of Life: A Study in Yoga
Morning Talks
Naam or Word
A Great Saint—Baba Jaimal Singh: His Life and Teachings
Jap Ji: The Message of Guru Nanak
Spiritual Elixir, Vols. I and II
The Teachings of Kirpal Singh (compiled by Ruth Seader)
   Vol. I: The Holy Path
   Vol. II: Self-Introspection/Meditation
   Vol. III: The New Life
Heart to Heart Talks—Vols. I and II (edited by Malcolm Tillis)
The Night Is a Jungle and Other Discourses of Kirpal Singh
Man! Know Thyself
Spirituality: What It Is
The Mystery of Death
The Wheel of Life: The Law of Action and Reaction
A Brief Life Sketch of Hazur Baba Sawan Singh Ji Maharaj
God Power, Christ Power, Guru Power
Seven Paths to Perfection
Simran: The Sweet Remembrance of God
How to Develop Receptivity

BY DARSHAN SINGH

The Cry of the Soul: Mystic Poetry
The Secret of Secrets: Spiritual Talks

BY OTHER AUTHORS

The Beloved Master, edited by Bhadra Sena
The Saint and His Master, by B.M. Sahai and R.K. Khanna
The Ocean of Grace Divine, edited by Bhadra Sena
Seeing Is Above All: Sant Darshan Singh's First Indian Tour,
   edited by H.C. Chadda
Kirpal Singh: The Story of a Saint,
   compiled and adapted for children; with illustrations
Portrait of Perfection: A Pictorial Biography of Kirpal Singh

OTHER BOOKS

Books listed on the preceding page may be ordered through your bookseller or directly from Sawan Kirpal Publications, Route 1, Box 24, Bowling Green, VA 22427, or Sawan Kirpal Publications, 2 Canal Road, Vijay Nagar, Delhi-110009, India.

SAT SANDESH: THE MESSAGE OF THE MASTERS

This monthly magazine is filled with practical and inspiring articles on all aspects of the mystic experience. Discourses by the living Master, Sant Darshan Singh, provide the initiate and seeker with invaluable information and guidance on meditation and the spiritual life. Also included are articles by Sant Kirpal Singh and Baba Sawan Singh. Poetry, photos, and other features appear in each issue. For subscription information write: Sat Sandesh, Subscription Dept., Route 1, Box 24, Bowling Green, VA 22427.

FURTHER INFORMATION

Mr. T.S. Khanna, General Representative, 8807 Lea Lane, Alexandria, VA 22309.

Olga Donenberg, Midwest Representative, 6007 N. Sheridan Rd., #14-B, Chicago, IL 60660.

Sunnie Cowen, Southern Representative, 3976 Belle Vista Dr. E., St. Petersburg Beach, FL 33706.

Sant Darshan Singh resides at Kirpal Ashram, 2 Canal Road, Vijay Nagar, Delhi-110009, India.